ISHAVASYA UPANISHAD

Swami Mukundananda is a world-renowned spiritual teacher, an international authority on mind management, and a bestselling author who earned his degrees from the prestigious IIT Delhi and IIM Calcutta. He worked with a multinational firm for a short while before renouncing a promising career to enter monkhood. He studied the Vedic scriptures at the feet of Jagadguru Kripaluji Maharaj. For four decades now, he has been sharing his vast knowledge through his books, lectures, and life-transformation lectures.

Every day, Swamiji meets hundreds, and even thousands, of people from all walks of life. His steadfast positivity exudes hope, clarity, and a sense of purpose to those who connect with him. He has deeply influenced the lives of millions who have been drawn by his profound integrity, charismatic personality, and passion to serve. Despite his hectic schedule, those who encounter him experience his warmth and compassion and feel deeply touched by his humility. Swamiji's lectures are humorous, his arguments are logical and well laid-out, and most of all, his advice is practical. His lectures on social media platforms are loved and followed by millions. Swamiji divides his time between India and the US.

swamimukundananda.org
facebook.com/Swami.Mukundananda
instagram.com/Swami_Mukundananda
linkedin.com/in/swamimukundananda
x.com/Sw_Mukundananda
youtube.com/c/swamimukundananda

Other Books by the Author

7 Divine Laws to Awaken Your Best Self
(Also available in Hindi)

7 Mindsets for Success, Happiness and Fulfilment
(Also available in Hindi, Gujarati, Marathi, Oriya and Telugu)

Bhagavad Gita: The Song of God

Golden Rules for Living Your Best Life

Nourish Your Soul: Inspirations from and Lives of Great Saints

Questions You Always Wanted to Ask

Science of Healthy Diet

Spiritual Dialectics

Spiritual Secrets from Hinduism: Essence of the Vedic Scriptures

The Art & Science of Happiness

The Power of Thoughts

The Science of Mind Management
(Also available in Gujarati and Telugu)

Yoga for the Body, Mind & Soul

Books for Children

Essence of Hinduism

Festivals of India

Healthy Body Healthy Mind: Yoga for Children

Inspiring Stories for Children (set of 4 books)

Mahabharat: The Story of Virtue and Dharma

My Best Friend Krishna

My Wisdom Book: Everyday Shlokas, Mantras, Bhajans and More

Ramayan: The Immortal Story of Duty and Devotion

Saints of India

ISHAVASYA UPANISHAD

Swami Mukundananda

RUPA

First published by
Rupa Publications India Pvt. Ltd
7/16 Ansari Road, Daryaganj
New Delhi 110002

Sales Centres
Bengaluru Chennai Hyderabad
Jaipur Kathmandu Kolkata Mumbai Prayagraj

H-ISBN: 978-93-6156-017-0
E-ISBN: 978-93-6156-968-5

First impression 2025

10 9 8 7 6 5 4 3 2 1

Printed in India

This commentary is dedicated to my beloved Spiritual Master, Jagadguru Shree Kripaluji Maharaj, who illuminated humankind with the purest rays of divine knowledge. He was immersed in the divine love and bliss of God and engaged in inundating the entire planet with it.

He compassionately engaged me in the service of the Supreme Divine Personality and guided me to spread the auspicious knowledge of the Vedic scriptures. This elucidation of the Ishavasya Upanishad, named Kripalu Toshini Teeka (commentary for the pleasure of my merciful Gurudev), has been written in the fulfillment of His instruction. I pray that by His blessings it will be helpful in guiding sincere seekers of the Absolute Truth on the path to enlightenment.

Contents

Introduction to the Upanishads	3
Introduction to Some Common Vedic Terms	17
Useful Note	21
Brief Introduction to the Ishavasya Upanishad	23
Shanti Path Mantra	27
Mantra 1	36
Mantra 2	42
Mantra 3	48
Mantra 4	54
Mantra 5	62
Mantra 6	68
Mantra 7	75
Mantra 8	81
Mantra 9	93
Mantra 10	103
Mantra 11	108
Mantra 12	114

Invocation

prathamam sadgurum vande śhrī kṛiṣhṇa tadanantaram
guruḥ paapātmanām trātā śhrī kṛiṣhṇastvamalātmanām

'I first offer my respectful obeisance to my gurudev, Jagadguru Shree Kripaluji Maharaj, and then to the Supreme Lord Shree Krishna. While Shree Krishna embraces the pure-hearted, my gurudev is so merciful that He offers shelter even to the spiritually destitute.'

mukundānanda prapannoham guru pādāravindayoḥ
tasya preraṇayā tasya divyādeśham vadāmyaham

'This insignificant inconsequential soul, who goes by the name of Mukundananda in the world, is surrendering at the lotus feet of his Spiritual Master. With his guru's permission, inspiration, and grace, he is humbly going to elucidate on spiritual topics.'

vande vṛindāvanānandām rādhikām parameśhvarīm
gopikām paramām śhūddhām hlādinīm śhakti rūpiṇīm

'I offer my respectful obeisance to Radha Rani, the Supreme Goddess and the bliss-giving power of God. She is the purest of the gopis and embodies the bliss of Vrindavan.'

kadā drakṣhyāmi nandasya bālakam nīpamālakam
pālakam sarva sattvānām lasattilaka bhālakam

'When will my eyes see the wonderful form of the Supreme Lord Shree Krishna, who appeared on this earth as the Son of Nand? He is adorned with a flower garland around His neck and the holy tilak mark on His forehead; He is the protector of virtuous people.'

ajāta pakṣhā iva mātaram khagāḥ
satanyam yathā vatsatarāḥ kṣhudhārtāḥ
priyam priyeva vyuṣhitam viṣhaṇṇā
manoravindākṣha didṛikṣhate tvām

'O Lord! As a baby bird yearns for its mother, as a famished infant longs to suckle the mother's breast, and as a lover craves for the beloved, may my mind always long for Your divine vision.'

Introduction to the Upanishads

The Upanishads reveal the nature of the Absolute Truth. They help us solve the mystery of life and creation. Who are we? Why are we on this planet? Why does creation exist? Is there a Supreme Intelligence behind creation? And what, after all, is the purpose of the world? On these bigger questions of life, the Upanishads provide astonishing insights. The knowledge they expound is unmatched in its sublimity. For this reason, these holy books are held in the highest esteem by spiritualists, thinkers, and philosophers.

The Supreme Brahman has revealed the Upanishads for the eternal well-being of the souls in this world. Apart from philosophic insights, they provide clear guidance on the methodologies for spiritual elevation. Their mantras are profound utterances, couched in poetic language that is direct and deep. They are eminently capable of guiding souls from their present state of material bondage to the perfection of God-realization.

Knowledge is the first step in the implementation of any technique. Without a clear understanding, we will grope and flounder in the dark. In ignorance, we will rely upon guesswork, experimentation, and hearsay. In fact, expert know-how can make the difference between success and failure. Even one little gem of wisdom can create a paradigm shift in life. Then what to speak of the treasure chest of wisdom that the Upanishads contain!

Emphasizing the supramental importance of wisdom, the Bhagavad Gita states:

sarvam jñāna-plavenaiva vṛijinam santariṣhyasi

(verse 4.36)

'By seating oneself on the boat of knowledge, one can cross over the ocean of material existence.'

The souls in this realm of maya are covered by the darkness of ignorance. From the Upanishads shines forth the bright light of wisdom before which nescience cannot remain. Let us situate ourselves on the ship of Upanishadic knowledge and sail over the samsara of life and death.

At the Feet of the Guru

The Upanishads were traditionally studied under the tutelage of enlightened masters, which is how they got their name. *Upa* means 'to go close' and *niṣhad* means 'to sit'. Hence, the word *Upanishad* implies 'knowledge gained at the feet of the guru'.

In the ancient Indian culture, aspirants endowed with curiosity to know the Absolute Truth would submissively approach a realized sage, who was well versed in Vedic learning and situated in divine consciousness. Seated at the feet of such a teacher, disciples would attentively study these holy books. On hearing the Truths with faith, they would contemplate upon the knowledge and imbibe it in their heart. Simultaneously, they would engage in intense spiritual practice and service to their guru, with a burning desire to experience God's limitless love.

Then one day, by their guru's grace, the disciples would find themselves established in the supreme realization. With gratitude to their spiritual teacher for the gift of divine wisdom, they would in turn accept students, and pass on their realizations to the next generation of seekers. In this way, the cycle of transmitting knowledge from guru to disciple continued in every era.

This one-on-one process of learning is the reason why some Sanskrit-English dictionaries explain the word ***Upanishad*** as meaning **'secret doctrine'**.[1] Likewise, the necessity of receiving wisdom at the guru's feet has led to another connotation for ***Upanishads*** as '**esoteric knowledge**', or 'that which is not openly available'.

With the invention of the printing press a few centuries ago, access to Upanishadic wisdom became more extensive. Since then, digital technology and the internet have made these holy texts even more accessible, and opened up possibilities for their widespread dissemination. In this modern scenario, the *Kripalu Toshini Teeka*, in your hands, has been penned for the benefit of all humankind.

Integral Portion of the Vedas

The Upanishads are an integral part of the sacred Vedas. It is important to note that the Vedic texts are not products of the human intellect. Rather, they are manifestations of the jnana shakti (knowledge energy) of the Supreme Brahman. Thus, they are eternal like God.

---

1 Monier-Williams, Monier, *A Sanskrit-English Dictionary*, New Edition, Motilal Banarsidass, New Delhi, 1986.

This leads to the question: 'How did these eternal scriptures appear in our world?' The answer is: *niḥśhvasitamasya vedāḥ* 'The Vedas were manifest by the breath of God.' The Shreemad Bhagavatam states along the same lines: *tene brahma hṛidā ya ādikavaye* (verse 1.1.1) 'The Vedas were initially revealed in the heart of Shree Brahma.' Subsequently, Brahmaji gave birth to many elevated sages by the power of his mind and entrusted the Vedic knowledge to them.

In previous ages, the Vedas were transmitted by oral tradition because of which they came to be known as *shruti,* meaning 'knowledge received through the ear'. This tradition continued till the end of *Dwapar Yug*. Then, Sage Krishna Dwaipayan compiled the Vedas in writing and divided them into four parts. Thenceforth, Sage Dwaipayan came to be known as Ved Vyas, 'the one who compiled and divided the Vedas'.

It is significant to note that Ved Vyas is never referred to as *Ved Rachayitā,* meaning 'writer of the Vedas'. Since the Vedas are *apauruṣheya,* or 'not created by any human', they are a trustworthy and reliable source of divine wisdom. In contrast are *pauruṣheya* books which are written by humans, and as a result, subject to some inherent limitations. These are discussed next.

The Four Pitfalls of Human Knowledge

All wisdom originating from a human source is vulnerable to four defects:

Karṇāpāṭava means 'limitations of the senses'. This is the first pitfall of human knowledge—the perception of our senses is restricted. For instance, the human eye cannot see objects that are too small. To increase its range, we use microscopes, and yet, atomic movement remains obscure.

Bhram means 'confusion caused by illusion'. It is the second human shortcoming. This illusion can be of two kinds: 1) mistaking one entity for another—for example, a bronze chain can be confused for a gold one; or 2) perceiving an entity where none exists—this is just as a mirage in the desert creates a perception of water, though there is none.

Pramāda, which means 'to make mistakes', is the third flaw in human knowledge. As the saying goes, 'To err is human.' For instance, doctors intend to prescribe one medicine, but accidentally write another on the patient's slip. Similarly, authors could be mistaken in their assumptions, arguments, interpretations, and conclusions.

Vipralipsā is the fourth defect in knowledge from a human source. It means 'the propensity to cheat'. This is the tendency to make false claims with the intention of deceiving others. Politicians over-exaggerate their achievements to impress voters. Even well-reputed scientists tamper with results of experiments to garner prestige.

These four weaknesses of human knowledge make its reliability questionable. Even scientific theories get refuted; they are superseded by newer and better ones. Thus, even if a book is authored by a genius, we cannot be sure it is flawless. The Vedas, however, being of divine origin, are free from the above vulnerabilities of mortals. Since God is without defects, the knowledge manifest by Him is also devoid of flaws. The *Manu*

Smriti therefore states:

> *bhūtam bhavyam bhaviṣhyam cha sarvam vedāt prasidhyati* (verse 12.97)

'The ultimate authority for determining the validity of any spiritual principle is the Vedas.'

Four Sections of the Vedas

Samhitā, *Brāhmaṇ*, *Āraṇyak*, and *Upanishads* are the four main segments of each Veda. The ***Samhitas*** contain mantras addressed to the Supreme Divine Personality and various celestial gods. The ***Brahman*** sections enunciate rituals for material rewards and promotion to heaven. The ***Aranyaks*** discuss the meanings of rituals, leading to metaphysical inquiry. The ***Upanishads*** reveal the nature of the Supreme, the 'self', and the world.

In every cluster of Vedic mantras, the Upanishads form the last section. Since *upasanghār* means 'conclusion', this is yet another explanation for their name.

Again, since they appear at the *ant* (end) in the Vedas, they are also known as ***Vedant***. Finally, the summary of all these individual Vedantas is the ***Vedant Sutra***, a famous philosophic text written in the form of aphorisms. It expounds upon the Supreme Brahman. Thus, it is also called ***Brahma Sutra***.

Going beyond Ritualistic Ceremonies

Most Vedic mantras deal with elaborate and difficult ritualistic ceremonies. Rarely do scholars in modern times have proper knowledge of such yajnas (fire sacrifices). The inadequate expertise and practice does not produce desired fruits. In fact, improperly done yajnas could even become a transgression and bestow adverse fruits. Hence, in the present age of Kali, people are dissuaded from performing the karm-kand (ritualistic ceremonies) activities of the Vedas.

The Upanishads, in contrast, do not concern themselves with any form of rituals. They restrict themselves to discussing profound philosophical truths. They do not detail the personal histories of rishis but delve into the workings of their mind. Keeping their focus on the bigger questions of life, they bestow deep spiritual insights.

The main topics of discussion in the Upanishads are God, the embodied souls, maya, and their relationship with one another. These sacred works also reveal esoteric secrets about the paths to the ultimate realization. Amazingly, even after so many millennia of changes in human society, the appeal of the Upanishads has persisted in modern times, and they continue to fascinate the intellects of profound thinkers and seekers.

Praise for the Upanishads

These sacred texts are held in high esteem not only in India but throughout the world. Profuse appreciation for them has been expressed by multitudes of Western scholars and thinkers.

On savouring their ambrosia-like wisdom, Arthur Schopenhauer, famous German philosopher, put the Upanishads on his head and began dancing. He wrote:

> In the whole world there is no study...so beneficial and elevating as that of the Upanishads. It has been the solace of my life, it will be the solace of my death![2]

Prof. Max Müller, the famous Sanskrit scholar from Germany, who initially misinterpreted Indian scriptures for a fee, later wrote:

> If these words of Schopenhauer required any endorsement I should willingly give it as the result of my experience during a long life devoted to study of many philosophies and many religions.[3]

The Austrian physicist, Erwin Schrödinger, wrote:

> There is obviously only one alternative, namely the unification of minds or consciousnesses. Their multiplicity is only apparent, in truth there is only one mind. This is the doctrine of the Upanishads.[4]

The poet, T.S. Eliot, was so inspired by his reading of the Upanishads that he based the final portion of his famous poem 'The Waste Land' upon them. Interestingly, the last lines of the poem are in Sanskrit:

> Datta. Dayadhvam. Damyata. Shantih shantih shantih[5]

---

2 Müller, F. Max, (ed.), *The Sacred Books of the East, Vol. 1*, The Clarendon Press, Oxford, 1900, p. lxi.

3 Woodroffe, Sir John, *Is India Civilized: Essays on Indian Culture*, Ganesh & Co., Madras, 1918, p. 112.

4 Schrödinger, Erwin, *What is Life with Mind and Matter and Autobiographical Sketches*, Cambridge University Press, 1st edition, 1962, Kindle e-book.

5 Eliot, T.S., *The Waste Land*, Boni and Liveright, New York, 1922, p. 49.

The Indologist, Friedrich Shlegel, wrote:

> Even the loftiest philosophy of the Europeans...appears, in comparison with the abundant light and vigour of Oriental idealism, like a feeble...spark in the full flood of heavenly glory of the noonday sun—faltering and feeble, and ever ready to be extinguished.[6]

Paul Deussen, a German philosopher, wrote:

> Eternal philosophic truth has seldom found a more striking and decisive expression than in the emancipating knowledge of the Upanishads.

The Total Number of Upanishads

There is a debate regarding the number of Upanishads. On the one hand, *Smarta sampradayas* claim there are 1031 Upanishads—one for each of the 1031 *shakhas* (branches) of the four Vedas. They believe that most of the original ones have been lost. On the other hand, *Vaishnav sampradayas* claim the number is 108.

Since the correct answer is hidden in the annals of history, it is difficult for us to arrive at a conclusion. However, we do know that there were 1031 *shakhas* of the Vedas, of which only 15 remain. The rest got destroyed with the passage of time. So, it does seem that many Upanishads existed besides the ones presently available. Scholars agree that currently there are around 220 Upanishads remaining on the earth.

---

[6] Müller, F. Max, *Three Lectures on the Vedanta Philosophy: Delivered at the Royal Institution in March 1894*, Longmans, Green, and Co., London, 1901, p. 11.

Of the available ones, Adi Shankaracharya outlined 11 as principal Upanishads for deep study. He opined these were sufficient for the realization of Brahman. On these 11, he wrote a commentary, now known as *Ekadashopanishad Shankarabhashya*. The 11 he selected are: *Ishavasya*, *Kena*, *Katha*, *Prashna*, *Mundaka*, *Manduka*, *Aitreya*, *Taittiriya*, *Shwetashvatar*, *Chhandogya*, and *Brihadaranyak Upanishads*.

Together, these 11 Upanishads form a part of the famous *Prasthan Trayi*, that are considered the most important triad amongst the Vedic scriptures.

Prasthan Trayi—Three Gateways to Vedic Learning

Though they are a reservoir of profound insights, the Vedas are not easy to comprehend. Therefore, to elaborate upon their teachings, sages composed many more scriptures. These include 6 Vedangas, 4 Upavedas, 18 Puranas, 2 Itihas, 6 Darshan Shastras, 100 Smritis, and thousands of Nibandhas. Together, these sacred texts are referred to as the 'Vedic scriptures'.

Compare this scenario to the Constitution of India. Lawyers have written hundreds of commentaries upon it. Their aim is not to refute the Constitution, but to explain its articles, parts, and schedules. Likewise, the supplementary Vedic scriptures do not deviate from the authority of the Vedas, rather, they elaborate upon them.

This, however, has led to an even more confounding problem. The compendium of scriptures is so numerous and vast that it is virtually impossible to read them all. So, where should one begin the journey of studying them?

Scholars commonly agree that there are three gateways to the colossal body of Vedic wisdom. These *Prasthan Trayi* are: 1) Brahma Sutras, 2) Bhagavad Gita, and 3) 11 major Upanishads.

It has become a tradition for founders of major schools of Vedant to write commentaries on the *Prasthan Trayi.* Shankaracharya, the founder of *Advaita vada*, wrote the *Shankarabhashya* on each of these, which continue to endure in popularity.

Madhvacharya, the founder of *Dvaita vada*, wrote commentaries on the *Brahma Sutras*, the Bhagavad Gita, and all the principal Upanishads. The *Anu Vyakhyana*, a supplement to his bhashya (commentary) on the *Brahma Sutras*, is the most famous of his works.

Ramanujacharya, the founder of *Vishishta Advaita vada*, wrote a commentary on *Brahma Sutras*, known as *Shree Bhashya.* He also wrote a bhashya on the Bhagavad Gita. In his lineage, commentaries on the principal Upanishads were written by Rangaramanuja.

Both Nimbarkacharya, the founder of *Dvaita Advaita vada*, and Vallabhacharya, the founder of *Vishuddh Advaita vada*, wrote commentaries on the *Brahma Sutras* and Bhagavad Gita. In these, they quoted hundreds of mantras from the Upanishads. However, they did not write individual commentaries on the principal Upanishads.

In the lineage of Chaitanya Mahaprabhu—the founder of *Achintya Bhedabheda vada*—commentaries were written a few centuries after him by Baladeva Vidyabhushan. He penned *Govind Bhashya* on the *Brahma Sutras* and *Gita Bhushan Teeka* on the Bhagavad Gita. His commentaries on the principal

Upanishads got lost over time; amongst them, only the *Ishopanishad Bhashya* remains.

Your lowly servant, author of this commentary, is a disciple of Jagadguru Shree Kripaluji Maharaj. This *Kripalu Toshini Teeka* of the *Ishavasya Upanishad* is based on the spiritual insights I received from Him.

About Jagadguru Shree Kripaluji Maharaj

He was a descended saint, who re-established the ancient Vedic knowledge in modern times. His devotees lovingly called him 'Maharajji'. At the young age of 34, Maharajji lectured for ten days in sophisticated Sanskrit, before the Kashi Vidvat Parishat, the supreme body of 500 Vedic scholars in the holy city of Kashi. Quoting masterfully from hundreds of Vedic scriptures, he revealed the simple straightforward path to God-realization for the present times.

When the esteemed body of erudite scholars realized that Kripaluji Maharaj's Vedic understanding was deeper than that of all of them together, they honoured him with the title of Jagadguru, or 'Spiritual Master of the World'. He thus became the fifth saint in Indian history to receive the original title of Jagadguru. The four personalities who received this title prior to him were Jagadguru Shankaracharya, Jagadguru Nimbarkacharya, Jagadguru Ramanujacharya, and Jagadguru Madhvacharya.

The phraseology used by the Kashi Vidvat Parishat, while acclaiming Kripaluji Maharaj as the fifth original Jagadguru in Indian history, is pertinent to note:

dhanyo mānya jagadgurūttama padaiḥ so 'yam samabhyarchte

'We are blessed to honour him as "Jagadguruttam", Supreme amongst the Jagadgurus.'

It was my extreme good fortune to learn the esoteric science of God-realization at the lotus feet of Jagadguruttam Shree Kripaluji Maharaj. Being of compassionate nature, He blessed me with abundant personal guidance and kind showers of affection, even though I was not eligible for it. With utmost indebtedness to my most merciful gurudev, I pray that the *Kripalu Toshini Teeka* of the *Ishavasya Upanishad* will be pleasing to Him.

Relationship between Knowledge and Devotion

A question often arises in the minds of seekers regarding the connection between knowledge and devotion. The following example provides an insight into the answer.

If you were given a diamond ring and told it was worth a hundred rupees, you would value it only to that extent. Instead, if a jeweller informed you that the diamond embedded in it was worth one crore rupees, you would be thrilled to have received the ring. The knowledge of its value would induce an appropriate amount of love for it.

Likewise, in spirituality as well, knowledge and loving devotion are interrelated. True knowledge of God naturally leads to love for Him. The Shreemad Bhagavatam states: *sā vidyā tanmatir yayā* (4.29.49) 'True knowledge is that which helps us develop love for God.'

So, while the Upanishads reveal the Absolute Truth, they also strongly urge the soul to cultivate devotion to the Lord. Verse 2.3.3 of the *Mundakopanishad* states: 'Take the bow of Upanishadic wisdom. On this great weapon, place the arrow of bhakti. Let bhav be the razor edge of the arrow. Then, go and hunt for the Supreme Brahman.'

Alas, in the last couple of centuries, the original bhashyas of the great sages have become obscure. They have been replaced in popularity by the commentaries of more recent scholars with incomplete knowledge and no appreciation of bhakti. Their commentaries have limited the Supreme Brahman to the Formless, which is merely one of His aspects. To establish their erroneous and often atheistic viewpoints, they have misconstrued the straightforward meanings of the mantras, creating complex and abstruse interpretations.

As a result, people have come to believe that the Upanishads can never be comprehended by them. Or that they are too dry to be savoured with relish. Some even fear reading the Upanishads, believing they will lose the little devotion they have for God. This commentary is being presented to remove such misconceptions. To firmly establish the Supreme Divine Personality as the summum bonum of the Upanishads. To rediscover the super-excellence of para bhakti (divine love). And to confirm God-realization as the ultimate goal of the souls in this world.

I hope the book will fulfill the sincere objective with which it has been published and help seekers in their quest for the Absolute Truth and in their journey to God-realization.

Introduction to Some Common Vedic Terms

The word meanings of a language reference the cultural and philosophical framework of the people who speak it. Sanskrit words, therefore, derive their meanings from the conceptual system of thought in India, which has been distinct from the Western thought that shaped meanings of English words.

This is why many Sanskrit terms do not have exact English equivalents as they express ideas in different settings. For example, there is no English word that accurately conveys the meaning of Brahman (the formless, attributeless, all-pervading aspect of God). The same problem typically arises with translating the word 'dharma' into English—the path of righteousness, one's incumbent duty, virtue, and prescribed duties—are all gross approximations of its meaning.

Thus, to retain the flavour of the idea being conveyed, many of the original Sanskrit terms have been retained. Such words and phrases have been included in the Glossary at the back of the book, with explanations. A few significant terms in the Vedic literature are explained here to help the reader easily grasp the concepts presented in the *Kripalu Toshini Teeka*.

Important Terms in Vedic Philosophy

Bhagavan (God): In the Vedas, 'God' refers to the One Supreme

Entity. He is all-powerful, all-knowing, and omnipresent. He is the Creator, Maintainer, and Annihilator of this world. He possesses innumerable contradictory attributes at the same time. Thus, He is both formless and possesses a form.

Avatar (Descension): Occasionally, by His causeless grace, God descends upon the earth and engages in divine pastimes (leelas) to uplift the souls. Such a descension is called 'Avatar'. The Sanskrit word is: *avataraṇan avatārah*, meaning 'one who descends from above'. Hence, 'Descension' is a more accurate English translation of the word than 'Incarnation'. Nevertheless, 'Avatar' is now a part of the English dictionary and can easily be used as it is.

Atma (soul): It is a tiny fragmental part of God. The soul is spiritual in nature, and hence distinct from the material body. The presence of the atma imparts consciousness to the body, which is made from insentient matter.

Jiva (embodied soul): The soul that is in the embodied state is called jivatma because it keeps the body *jīvit* (alive). These words—atma and jiva—are interchangeably used while referring to souls in the material realm.

Punar janma (rebirth): According to the Vedic understanding, the soul neither originated on birth, nor will it be destroyed when the body dies. What we term as death in worldly parlance is merely the soul discarding its old body, to move on to a new one. It is not free to choose its next birth; that is decided by God based upon the Law of Karma.

Paramatma (Supreme Soul): Along with the individual soul (jivatma), God is also seated within the body. He is called

Paramatma (Supreme Soul). He accompanies the jivatma life after life, into whichever bodily form it goes. The Paramatma does not interfere with the activities of the living entity but remains a silent Witness. The jivatma is forgetful of its eternal friend and is struggling to enjoy the material energy.

Maya (material nature): The material energy, called prakriti, is not antithetical to God; rather, it is one of His innumerable powers. At the time of dissolution, prakriti remains latent within the being of God. When He wishes to create the world, He glances at it, and it begins to unwind from its latent state. It then manifests the various gross and subtle elements of creation.

Samsara (cycle of life and death): While one aspect of maya creates the world, its second aspect is instrumental in keeping the souls bound to the repeated cycle of life and death, called samsara. Maya makes us forget our identity as divine souls and puts us under the illusion of being the material body. This is why we pursue bodily pleasures in the world.

Why has the material energy, maya, enveloped us in the first place? This is because we have turned away from God. He is of the nature of light, while the material energy is of the nature of darkness. One who turns away from light is naturally overcome by darkness. Likewise, the souls who have turned their backs towards Him are covered by material energy.

Yog (union with God): After innumerable lifetimes of endeavouring in the material realm, the soul comes to the realization that the infinite divine bliss it seeks will not be attained from the world but from God. Then, it must follow the path of *Yog* to reach the stage of perfection. When the soul achieves perfect union with God, it becomes liberated from the clutches of the material energy. *Yog* refers both to the spiritual pathway to God and to the state of union with Him.

Gunas (modes of Nature): The material energy has three constituent modes: sattva, rajas, and tamas. These gunas exist in varying proportions in our personality and influence us.

- ***tamo guna*** (mode of ignorance) induces laziness, stupor, ignorance, anger, violence, and addiction, thereby pulling the soul deeper into the darkness of material illusion.
- ***rajo guna*** (mode of passion) inflames the desires of the mind and senses and induces one to endeavour passionately for fulfilling worldly ambitions.
- ***sattva guna*** (mode of goodness) illumines a person with knowledge and nourishes virtuous qualities, such as kindness, patience, and tolerance. It makes the mind peaceful and suitable for spiritual practice.

Sadhana (spiritual practice): The spiritual discipline a sadhak undertakes for elevation of the soul and attainment of the supreme goal.

Sadhak (spiritual practitioner): One who practises spiritual disciplines for the elevation of their soul.

Useful Note

The *Ishavasya Upanishad* opens with an invocation, followed by 18 mantras. For all 19 verses, the *Kripalu Toshini Teeka* has been organized in the following manner:

Sanskrit Verse. The original Sanskrit mantra is presented in Devanagari script.

Transliteration. The same verse is presented in English script with diacritical marks denoting the exact pronunciation.

Word Meanings. The English meanings of individual Sanskrit words and phrases are given.

Translation. Next comes the English meaning of the Sanskrit verse.

Commentary. This is the *Kripalu Toshini Teeka* explanation of the mantra.

For the Scholars. This section has been added to some mantras. It contains content of academic interest as an addendum to the commentary. This gives the reader the option to skip it on the first reading and still understand most of the book. One could then come back to this section in subsequent readings to explore the subject in more detail.

Link. At the end of the commentary to a mantra and prior to the next one, you will find a short italicized paragraph. It helps the reader establish the link to the subject matter of the subsequent mantra.

Diacritical marks have been used with Sanskrit words to depict their exact pronunciation. Diacritics have not been used with Sanskrit words that are now a part of English language, such as 'samsara'. Again, for the sake of elegance of presentation and ease of reading, diacritical marks have not been used for many proper nouns as well, such as 'Shree Krishna'.

Glossary. Where Sanskrit words do not have equivalent English phrases that convey the meaning accurately, the original Sanskrit terms have been retained. These have been included in the 'Glossary' at the back of the book with detailed explanations. Sometimes for ease of reading, directly after the word, its meaning is presented in brackets.

Pronunciation Guide for English transliterations is provided in the appendices.

Index of Verses Quoted in the commentary is also presented in the appendices.

Brief Introduction to the Ishavasya Upanishad

This sacred text is considered the first Upanishad in the Vedic structure. Its name, *ishavasya*, is as beautiful as it is profound. The word *īśhā* means 'by God', while the extension *vāsya* means 'to pervade'. When combined, it has such a beautiful meaning: 'The Upanishad of the all-pervading God.' Using the root *īśhā*, scholars also refer to the scripture as *Isha Upanishad*, or in short, as *Ishopanishad*.

The Vedas are comprised of three sections: karm-kand (ritualistic ceremonies), jnana-kand (philosophic dissertation), and upasana-kand (devotion and worship). Interestingly, the *Ishopanishad* presents a beautiful summary of all three sections together.

This powerful role of the *Ishavasya Upanishad* stems from its location in the Vedas. It forms the 40th and last chapter of the *Kanva Shakha* of the *Shukla Yajur Veda*. The first 39 chapters are majorly concerned with karm-kand and minorly with jnana-kand. The *Ishopanishad* concerns itself with encapsulating them and the subsequent upasana-kand. Therefore, it summarizes the essence of the three main Vedic branches—karm, jnana, and bhakti.

Though one of the smallest, the *Ishavasya Upanishad* is amongst the most popular of the Upanishads. Mahatma Gandhi wrote powerful words of praise for it:

> If all the Upanishads and all the other scriptures happened all of a sudden to be reduced to ashes, and if only the first verse in the *Ishopanishad* were left in the memory of the Hindus, Hinduism would live forever.[7]

This sacred text is verily the essence of the 11 primary Upanishads. It begins by declaring the perfection of the Creator, and then draws an insightful corollary: Since God is perfect and complete, the world created by Him is also complete. Creation is perfectly designed to provide souls the opportunity to evolve towards the ultimate perfection.

As the 'Upanishad of the all-pervading God', the prime topic the *Ishopanishad* discusses is, naturally, God and God-consciousness. We find in it a description of the Supreme Divine Personality from many different contexts. To convey God's inconceivable and immeasurable attributes, it uses powerful comparisons and literary tools. Yet, it clarifies that even powerful celestials, such as Indra and Vayu, cannot fully know the Supreme, Who precedes all creation.

The *Ishopanishad* reminds us that having attained human birth, our primary duty is to attain the supreme destination of our soul. Forgetful of this, many fall prey to seeking the fleeting pleasures of the world. They expend their soul energy in sinful deeds. The Upanishad sternly warns such humans that a hellish abode awaits them in the afterlife if they continue in sinful pleasure-seeking activities.

We are then explained how to go about our everyday life with

---

7 Easwaran, Eknath, *The Upanishads*, 2nd edition, Nilgiri Press, USA, 2009, Kindle e-book.

the correct mindset. Material consciousness is characterized by thinking thus, 'I am the proprietor of all I possess. Everything here is for my enjoyment.' In contrast, spiritual consciousness is characterized by thoughts like, 'God is the Owner and Enjoyer of this entire world. I am merely His dedicated servant. I must use all I have in the service of the Almighty.' The Upanishad reassures us that work performed in this kind of spiritual consciousness will not bind us in maya, since the intention is not selfish.

The uniqueness of the *Ishopanishad* is that it takes up extreme and apparently contrary viewpoints and skillfully resolves them. In the process, it provides us the wisdom to achieve a harmonious balance among the different dimensions of life. We are informed of the need for cultivating both the spiritual and material aspects of life. In the same vein, we are asked not to reject either of the two realms—God and the world. With a proper mindset, both these spheres are important and add value to our life.

We should remind ourselves that God is sitting within every atom of creation. See all visible phenomena in the world—whether among sentient or insentient entities—as arising out of His pervasiveness. When we perceive this 'grand unity' of all beings with God, it will dispel the illusion of their independent existence. It is then that we will develop equanimity of vision.

The *Ishopanishad*, in its later portion, goes deep into bhakti, emphasizing the upasana-kand of the Vedas. It presents the devotee's yearning for a vision of the personal form of God, which he perceives as covered by effulgent light. Subsequently, as prayerful longing for God increases, the devotee appeals to the Lord for mercy that all impediments preventing his supreme ascension be burnt. He also prays for similar grace upon all living beings.

Come, let us now understand the mantras of this incomparable Upanishad. They are imbued with a host of sublime spiritual truths expressed succinctly.

Shanti Path Mantra

ॐ पूर्णमदः पूर्णमिदं पूर्णात् पूर्णमुदच्यते।
पूर्णस्य पूर्णमादाय पूर्णमेवावशिष्यते॥
ॐ शान्तिः शान्तिः शान्तिः॥

oṁ pūrṇamadaḥ pūrṇamidam pūrṇāt pūrṇamudachyate
pūrṇasya pūrṇamādāya pūrṇamevāvaśhiṣhyate
oṁ śhāntiḥ śhāntiḥ śhāntiḥ

oṁ—sacred syllable representing the formless aspect of God; *pūrṇam*—perfect and complete; *adaḥ*—that; *pūrṇam*—complete; *idam*—this; *pūrṇāt*—complete; *pūrṇam*—complete; *udachyate*—having emanated from; *pūrṇasya*—of the complete; *pūrṇam*—completely, all; *ādāya*—subtract; *pūrṇam*—complete; *eva*—even; *avaśhiṣhyate*—remains.

The Supreme Brahman is perfect and complete. This world, having emanated from Him, is also complete. Anything that the perfect and complete God manifests is complete as well. Having manifested the world, His completeness remains unchanged.

This *Shanti Path Mantra* bestows in one sweep an encapsulation of Upanishadic thought. The same mantra also appears in the *Brihadaranyak Upanishad* 5.1.1. The verse begins by declaring the perfection of the Creator. Let us probe it gradually.

Definition of God. To this often-asked question, Sage Parashar provides a beautiful answer. Using the completeness of God to define Him, he says in the *Vishnu Puran*:

aiśhvaryasya samagrasya dharmasya yaśhasaḥ śhriyaḥ
jñāna-vairāgyayośhchaiva ṣhaṣhṇām bhaga itīṅganā

(verse 6.5.74)

'God is He who possesses six opulences to unlimited extent—infinite strength, infinite knowledge, infinite beauty, infinite fame, infinite opulence, and infinite renunciation.'

In the above definition, Maharshi Parashar has enumerated six glories of God. It does not mean these are the only opulences the Supreme possesses. Factually, the Lord is replete with infinite glories and each to an infinite extent.

God's limitless glories are expressed in the *Shiv Mahimna Stotra* so charmingly, by admitting the inability to describe them. It states:

asita-giri-samam syāt kajjalam sindhu-pātre,
sura-tarūvara-śhākhā lekhanī patramurvī
likhati yadi gṛihītvā śhāradā sarvakālam
tadapi tava guṇānāmīśha pāram na yāti (verse 32)

'Assume the entire earth were employed as paper; all the trees from the celestial abodes were used as pens; and the oceans provided mountains-full of black ink. With all these at her disposal, if Saraswati were to write for endless aeons, she would still be unable to complete the description of the glories of God.'

The indescribable nature of the Supreme is likewise depicted by other great saints and scriptures. In verse 11.4.2, the Shreemad Bhagavatam beautifully conveys the futility of counting the virtues of God: 'God is endless, and His qualities are uncountable. Those who believe they will enumerate His infinite virtues possess a childish intellect. The grains of sand on the crust of the earth may somehow be estimated, but virtues of the Lord will forever remain uncountable.'

The mathematics of infinity is very interesting. It can give us a peek into the logic of the above *Shanti Path Mantra*. From infinity, if we subtract ten, we are still left with infinity. If we subtract a million, what remains is still infinite. But what if we subtract infinity from infinity? The answer is 'undefined'. It could be anything, depending upon the nature of the two infinities.

In the case of God, His infinitude is so immensely limitless that if you subtract infinity from Him, it will not reduce His personality in any way. Such is the nature of the Supreme Absolute. This idea was graphically portrayed by Anne Sexton, a Pulitzer Prize winner, in her poem 'What the Bird with the Human Head Knew':

> Then the well spoke to me.
> It said: Abundance is scooped from abundance,
> Yet abundance remains.[8] [9]

Materialistic consciousness fosters the idea of limited resources leading to a paradigm of scarcity. Success is then perceived as a limited pie, in which, if one person gets a share, it leaves less for others. Hence, humankind is destined to perpetually fight for diminishing resources. However, spiritual consciousness replaces the idea of a limited pie with the concept of abundance in the dominion of God, where there is enough for everyone to succeed.

---

8 Sexton, Anne, *The Complete Poems*, Houghton Mifflin, Boston, 1981.

9 https://sacompassion.net/poem-what-the-bird-with-the-human-head-knew-by-anne-sexton/. Last accessed on 15 March 2025.

Completeness of creation. As soon as we become aware of the world, the intellect begins to question: From where did this world arise? Who made it? Why was it made? What is its purpose? The *Shanti Path Mantra* gives us a starting point for the answers. It states that a supremely intelligent God created it for a divine purpose.

Since the Creator is infinitely complete, the world manifested by Him is also complete. And in manifesting it, the Creator does not diminish in any way. Thus, He creates infinite universes without depleting His energy or power.

The question then arises: if there is much misery in the world, how can we say it is 'complete'? We witness living beings undergoing birth, death, old age, and disease. Besides, there are countless other sufferings, tribulations, and miseries. How can such a sorrowful world be perfect, when its living beings are steeped in hardships? This question pricks the intellect and needs to be addressed.

The completeness of creation does not mean it is free from suffering. It simply implies that the world is self-sufficient for the purpose for which it was made. Its chief objective is to nurture the evolution of the indwelling souls to superconsciousness over a continuum of lifetimes. Creation is perfectly designed to provide souls the opportunity to evolve towards the ultimate perfection. To this end, the world sometimes becomes the 'School of Hard Knocks'. Understand through this analogy.

Eagles living in the Rocky Mountains build nests at a height of 5000 feet. For this, they use thorny ironwood to resist the strong winds that blow at such high altitudes. They lace their nest with cotton and leaves. When the eggs hatch, the mother and father eagles get busy bringing fodder for their chicks. But as the chicks grow, the nest becomes too tight. So, the mother eagle starts removing the padding in the nest, not because she is cruel, but because the chicks need to grow further. Feeling uncomfortable in the nest, the chicks emerge onto the cliff.

The parents continue caring for them, until one day, the mother lures her little one to the edge of the cliff and shoves it over. The poor baby enters into a free fall and to break its speed, it spreads its wings. It then begins doing what is most natural for eagles, which is to glide in the skies as the king of the birds.

If it were not for the mother's harsh push, the baby bird left on its own would have continued sitting on the cliff. Likewise, Creation continously challenges us, making us grow in the face of adversities. As a result, our consciousness slowly unfolds as our soul learns to soar higher and higher. Like this, we have been journeying since numerous lifetimes.

The purpose of the Universe is to present a field of possibilities to the materially bound souls—to aspire, strive, and act. Living in the material realm, we perform karmas and reap fruits, as per the universal Laws of Creation. Through the experiences of happiness and distress, success and failure, our soul keeps learning and evolving.

Sometimes, along our spiritual journey, we take a few steps back. At other times, we stop, dejectedly exclaiming, 'Enough! I cannot strive any further.' Then again, we continue forward. The search for happiness keeps nudging our soul, ensuring we keep striving forward. This yearning for happiness in our soul will only quieten when we reach the goal God has designed for us.

In this grand design of the Universe, pain plays an important role. The sign of a perfected soul is not the absence of pain. On the contrary, it is the ability to stay equipoised in the midst of it. Along these lines, the Bhagavad Gita states:

duḥkheṣhv-anudvigna-manāḥ sukheṣhu vigata-spṛihaḥ
vīta-rāga-bhaya-krodhaḥ sthita-dhīr munir uchyate

(verse 2.56)

'One whose mind remains undisturbed amidst misery, who does not crave pleasure, and who is free from attachment, fear, and anger, is called a sage of steady wisdom.' Thus, even suffering can become a catalyst for progress.

A question may be raised here. The word *adaḥ* in the mantra refers to God, while *idam* refers to the world. However, in the world, the jivas also reside. They have originated from the Supreme as well. Are the souls perfect as well?

The answer to this question is a matter of perspective. A six-month-old baby in her mother's womb may appear imperfect to others—its limbs and organs are not yet fully developed. But for the mother, the baby is perfect even in its present state. Likewise, in the eyes of God, all souls are His eternal fragments. They have been perfectly created by Him, and He has endowed them with potential to reach their supreme destination.

It is important to note that when we speak of the soul as 'complete', we are referring to their divine essence. In fact, the intrinsic essence of each soul is consciousness and bliss. The Vedas state: *chinmātram śhrīhareranśham sūkṣhmamakṣharamavyayam* 'The soul, as a fragment of God, is sentient, indestructible, and immutable.' The only difference is that the soul is tiny, while God is limitless.

For the Scholars

The powerful philosophical principle stated in this mantra leads to some other very important conclusions.

1) **God is both formless and possesses a form.** God's infinitude can lead to a question: If the Supreme is immeasurable, then can He have a form? If He has form, will He not be restricted to a particular area?

The doubt is easily resolved when we realize that the Lord is not limited to one kind of manifestation. In fact, to say that God cannot have a form, is to place a limit on Him. With a little thought, there should be no room for doubt that the all-powerful God can simultaneously be all-pervading and also exist in a personal form. The Vedas also support this notion.

dve vāva brahamaṇo rūpe mūrtam chaivāmūrtam cha

(*Brihadaranyak Upanishad* 2.3.1)

'The Supreme Entity possesses both a personal form and a formless aspect.'

2) **All avatars are perfect and complete.** A debate sometimes ensues amongst devotees of different forms of the Supreme. One claims, 'Krishna is bigger', the other refutes, 'No, Ram is bigger', while a third states, 'Shiv is the biggest'. However, this mantra helps us understand that all avatars of God are perfect

and complete. This is stated by Ved Vyas, who was Himself an avatar of the Supreme.

sarve pūrṇāḥ śhāśhvatāśhcha dehāstasyaparamātmanaḥ
(*Varaha Puran* 2.1.224)

'All descensions of God are replete with all divine powers.' Hence, we should not differentiate one avatar as bigger and another as smaller.

Whenever God descends in this world, He has certain objectives to accomplish. Accordingly, He manifests certain shaktis (powers) to perform specific leelas. The remaining shaktis remain latent. Hence, Ved Vyas states again in the *Varaha Puran*: *sarve sarvaguṇaiḥ pūrṇāḥ* (verse 2.1.245) 'All avatars of the Supreme Divine Lord are complete with infinite divine qualities.'

3) **Mention of avatars in the Vedas.** Some Vedic scholars opine that the Vedas do not describe the avatars and the personal forms of God. They claim such mentions are only in the Puranas. In fact, however, the Vedas have many such references. The *Rig Veda* states:

vishṇornu kam vīryāṇi pra vocham yaḥ pārthivāni
vimame rajāmsi (1.154.1)

'I now declare the mighty works of Bhagavan Vishnu, Who descended on the earth (in His avatars).'

In the following mantra, the *Rig Veda* uses the word *kucharaḥ*, where *ku* means 'earth' and *charaḥ* means 'moves around'. It states:

pra tadvishṇu stavate vīryeṇa mṛigo na bhīmaḥ kucharo
girishṭhāḥ (1.154.2)

'That Vishnu affirms His mightiness like a fierce lion. He descends on the earth, while His lair is in high places.'

The *Atharva Veda* uses the word *Sūkar*, in reference to Bhagavan Varaha. It states:

varāheṇa pṛithivī samvidānā sūkarāya vi jihīte mṛigāya
(verse 12.1.48)

'Repositioned in its orbit by Bhagavan Varaha, the earth upholds all living beings upon itself.'

Again, going back to the *Rig Veda*, where it mentions Bhagavan Vaman, stating:

yasyoruṣhu triṣhu vikramaṇeṣhvadhikṣhiyanti bhuvanāni viśhvā (*Vishnu Sooktam* 27)

'Trivikram Bhagavan (Vaman) measured the three worlds in three of His steps.'

Bhagavan Shiv is mentioned in the *Mahamrityunjaya Mantra* of the *Rig Veda*:

oṁ tryambakam yajāmahe sugandhim puṣhṭivardhanam
urvārukamiva bandhanān mṛityormukṣhīya māmṛitāt
(verse 7.59.12)

'We meditate on Bhagavan Shiv, the three-eyed God, Who is joyfully fragrant; He sustains and nourishes all. As a ripened fruit falls effortlessly to the ground, may He liberate us from the bondage of death and bestow immortality.'

Having clarified important concepts regarding the nature of the Creator, His creation, and the soul, let us now proceed to the first mantra of the Ishopanishad.

Mantra 1

ॐ ईशा वास्यमिदं सर्वं यत्किञ्च जगत्यां जगत् ।
तेन त्यक्तेन भुञ्जीथा मा गृधः कस्यस्विद्धनम् ॥ १॥

oṁ īśhā vāsyamidaṁ sarvam yatkiñcha jagatyām jagat
tena tyaktena bhuñjīthā mā gṛidhaḥ kasyasviddhanam

oṁ—sacred syllable representing the formless aspect of God; *īśha*—by God; *āvāsyam*—pervaded; *idam*—this; *sarvam*—all; *yat kiñcha*—whatever; *jagatyām*—all of creation; *jagat*—all that is sentient or insentient; *tena*—by him; *tyaktena*—renouncing; *bhuñjīthāḥ*—the desire for enjoyment; *mā*—do not; *gṛidhaḥ*—thirst for; *kasya svit*—of anyone; *dhanam*—treasures.

All of creation, whether sentient or insentient, is pervaded by God. Therefore, renouncing the desire for pleasure, stop thirsting for possessions; the world and its treasures have never belonged to anyone.

The most important word in this mantra is the first one, *īśhāvāsyam*, from which the Upanishad has derived its name. *Īśhā* means 'by God'. From the root *vas*, comes *vās*, which has four major meanings:

***Vās* means 'to reside'**. God lives in the entire world and in the heart of each jiva (soul).

***Vās* means 'to wear clothes'**. God is so immense that He wears the entire world as His garment. That is why sometimes He is called *Digambar*, the One Who, being so vast, wears 'directions' as His clothes.

***Vās* means 'to veil thickly'**. God has covered Himself by the three gunas of maya—sattva, rajas, and tamas. Hence, though we live in the world, we have no perception of Him.

***Vās* means 'to pervade'**. God is sitting within every atom of creation. Any phenomenon visible in the world—whether among sentient or insentient entities—arises from His pervasiveness.

The essence of all four interpretations is that God pervades the entire world. This implies that God does not simply make the world. Rather, having created it, He then takes up residence within every speck of it. Thus, He is often referred to as *ghata-ghata vāsī*, meaning 'One Who resides in every little particle.' Highlighting His all-pervading presence, the Puranas relate the following story of Nrisingh Bhagavan.

The demon king, Hiranyakashipu, was fed up with his son Prahlad's devotion, and asked him, kvāsau? *'Where is this God that you worship?'*

Prahlad responded, saḥ sarvatra *'Father, He is everywhere.' To illustrate his point, Prahlad pointed in four places, 'God resides in you. He resides in me. He lives in this blade of grass. And He also stays in this stone pillar.'*

Hiranyakashipu questioned, kasmāt stambhe na dṛiśhyate? *'If God is in the stone pillar, then why can I not see Him?' Saying this, he boxed the pillar.*

At that time, the pillar broke and God manifested from it in the form of Nrisingh avatar. Through this divine leela, the Lord revealed that He actually resides everywhere.

The mantra invites us to use the awareness of God's all-pervasiveness for changing our perspective towards the world. Since it is permeated by Bhagavan, we should not look upon worldly things as objects for our enjoyment. Instead, we should do *tena tyaktena*, 'become detached from the hankering of material enjoyment'. In its place, we must cultivate the habit of seeing the presence of the Divine in everything.

The mantra then concludes by saying, 'Remember, the world is not yours.' Let us understand this statement next. All theistic believers accept that God is the Creator, but the question still remains, 'What was the material He used to make the world? Where did the material come from? And who made that material?' Most philosophical systems remain clueless or at best give incomplete answers.

The Vedic scriptures, however, discuss this point with authority. They explain that when the Supreme wishes to create the world, He manifests the material energy from within His *mahodar* (enormous stomach). He then glances at maya with the intent of creating. His potent glance causes maya to begin unravelling. One by one, material entities begin to manifest, and the world comes into being. In this way, God literally creates the world from within Himself and sets it into motion.

It is thus not incorrect to say that God Himself becomes the world. Accordingly, the *Purush Sooktam* states: *puruṣha aevedam sarvam* 'God is everything that exists.' And the Bhagavad Gita (7.19) states: *vāsudevaḥ sarvamiti* 'All that exists is Vasudev.' Along the same lines, the *Chatushloki Bhagavatam* declares:

ahamevāsamevāgre nānyad yat sadasat param
paśhchādaham yadetachcha yo 'vaśhiṣhyeta so 'smyaham
(Shreemad Bhagavatam 2.9.33)

The verse explains that before creation, the Supreme alone existed. Even His material energy came later. All that exists now is His very form. And upon dissolution, He alone will remain.

Considering the world's divine origin, we are guided to replace our mindset of 'possessiveness' with the attitude of 'the world is God's property'. Whenever we make things, we start with God's materials. Factually, we do not make even an atom from scratch. Therefore, to consider ourselves as the owner of anything is pride fuelled by ignorance.

True knowledge frees us from the sense of ownership. If everything belongs to God, it is meant for His pleasure. With this spirit of service, we should use the things of the world. This is the sentiment expressed in the *Naivedya Mantra*:

tvadiyam vastu govind tubhyameva samarpaye
(*Harivansh Puran*)

'O Shree Krishna, all things are Yours. We received them from You and are offering them back unto You.'

In fact, seeking pleasure in material things is what binds us. The Bhagavad Gita states:

yajña-śhiṣhṭāśhinaḥ santo muchyante sarva-kilbiṣhaiḥ
bhuñjate te tvagham paapā ye pachantyātma-kāraṇāt
(verse 3.13)

'The spiritually-minded, who eat food that is first offered in sacrifice, are released from all kinds of sin. Others, who cook for their own enjoyment, verily eat only sin.' Here, Shree Krishna uses the word *bhuñjate* to convey, 'Do not try to enjoy the food; instead eat as an act of devotion.'

When we develop the proper perspective, we realize that the things of the world are neither good nor bad; the manner in which we use them determines their value. For example, a knife is neither destructive nor constructive. In the hands of a surgeon, the scalpel becomes an instrument for saving lives, while in the hands of a robber, the knife is used to take lives. Similarly, technology is neither a bane nor a boon; it can be utilized equally for good or bad purposes. Laptops, mobiles, and digital media can be employed to propagate the word of God, but they can also be used for racketeering, gambling, and frivolous fun.

The key message of the mantra is, therefore, to renounce the desire for enjoying things for ourselves. *Tyaktena bhuñjīthāḥ* implies: 'Give up the desire for pleasure and replace it with the spirit of "serving" the Supreme.'

For the Scholars

Is the world *mithya* (a non-existent entity)? A debate regarding the nature of the world is longstanding in Indian philosophy. The jnani followers of *Advaita* firmly believe that the world is an illusion. *Brahma satyam jaganmithyā jīvo brahmaiva nāparaḥ,* meaning 'Brahman is real, the world is false, and the jiva is non-different from Brahman.'

The Vaishnav acharyas refute this by asking the question, 'If the world is *mithya*, then how was it created?'

The jnanis respond by saying, 'It is *manaḥ kalpita*, a creation of the mind, due to our ignorance. When we dispel our ajnana (ignorance) and get situated in jnana, the world will cease to exist.'

However, the answer is not convincing because even great jnanis who had attained Brahma jnana continued to use the world. They utilized the paper and pencil of the world to write their books. This proves the world did not cease for them.

Further, after attaining Brahma jnana, great saints continue eating the food of this world. Shankaracharya's commentary on the *Brahma Sutra* 1.1.1 states: *paśhvādibhiḥ chāviśheṣhāt* 'Even a paramhansa feels hungry, as animals do.' The nourishment needs of the body must be met. Why should this be so if the world is *mithya*?

Again, the question arises that creation is so complex—from the tiniest atoms to the biggest galaxies. If it is *manaḥ kalpita*, how did our mind make such an astonishing world? Besides, if it is made with our mind, then everyone should have created dissimilar things. We see that even when a person dies, the world remains. So, how can it be a creation of one's mind?

This very first mantra of the *Ishopanishad* puts the matter to rest. It says, 'The entire world is pervaded by God.' Thus, there is no question of the world being a *mithya* or non-existent entity.

The external and internal worlds. Jagadguru Kripaluji Maharaj reconciled the jnani and Vaishnav views by explaining that there are two sansars (worlds). One is the external world, created by God. It cannot be *mithya* because it is made by the *satya* (eternally existent) God.

There is, in fact, another sansar that is *mithya*. This is the inner world within us—the world created by our own mind. It is our inner world that is the reason for our bondage.

Thus, for *vairagya* (detachment) we must finish the internal sansar. Many are under the illusion that the external world is the reason for their misery. They leave it, to reside in the Himalayas, yet strife continues. Instead, if they aimed to purify their mind, then even while living in the world, they would not be bound by it. In fact, the all-pervading nature of God in the world would come in their experience. Such is the verdict of the realized saints.

Hence, the gopis said: *jita dekhūṅ tita śhyāmamayī hai*

Hanumanji experienced: *siyarāmamaya saba jaga jānī*

After introducing us to the idea of seeing the presence of God in the world and not mis-utilizing it, the next mantra clarifies that we should not shy away from life. It encourages us to utilize our precious human birth by working in the proper spirit.

Mantra 2

कुर्वन्नेवेह कर्माणि जिजीविषेच्छतं समाः ।
एवं त्वयि नान्यथेतोऽस्ति न कर्म लिप्यते नरे ॥ २॥

kurvanneveha karmāṇi jijīviṣhechchhatam samāḥ
evam tvayi nānyatheto 'sti na karma lipyate nare

kurvan—performing; *eva*—thus; *iha*—during the life span;

karmāṇi—duties; *jijīviṣhet*—one should aspire to live; *śhatam*—one hundred; *samāḥ*—years; *evam*—living like this; *tvayi*—unto God; *na*—not; *anyathā*—else; *itaḥ*—from this; *asti*—there is; *na*—not; *karma*—work; *lipyate*—binding; *nare*—unto a human.

Human beings should aspire to live a hundred years, while performing their duties with the proper attitude. Work done for the pleasure of God will not result in karmic bondage. In fact, there is no simpler means for getting rid of the bonds of karma.

Our soul has been transmigrating amongst the 8.4 million species of life, on earth and on other planets. Once in a while, by the grace of God, the jiva receives the human form. This provides it with a golden chance to attain the supreme goal. The *Kenopanishad* states:

iha chedavedīdatha satyamasti
na chedihāvedīnmahatī vinaṣhṭiḥ (mantra 2.5)

'The human birth is a rare opportunity. If you do not utilize it to achieve your goal, you will suffer great ruin.'

The mantra says we must make the most of this opportunity by aspiring to live for a 100 years. This is the lifespan Nature has bestowed on humans in the age of Kali. Those who follow the rules of healthy living can expect to live for this long. Hence, when a boy receives the sacred thread, he is blessed that he may live a hundred years.

The word *jijīviṣhā* has been used, meaning 'the will to live'. By invoking a desire to live long, the mantra does not shy us away from life. In fact, it encourages us to do karma. The word *aeva* is for emphasis, 'definitely'. Thus, *kurvan aeva* means 'definitely do your work'. Spirituality should not be construed as a means of escapism. Swami Vivekananda's famous words are: 'Awake! Arise! And stop not, till the goal is reached.'[10] This is a translation of the *Kathopanishad* mantra: *uttiṣhṭhata jāgrata prāpya varānnibodhata* (1.2.4).

However, the quality of life is even more significant than the number of years lived. We must not waste our time in purposeless entertainment, instead we must use each precious moment for the highest benefit. Devarshi Narad, in his namesake scripture *Narad Bhakti Darshan*, says: *kṣhaṇādharmapi vyartham na neyam* 'Do not waste even half a moment of your invaluable human life.'

The mantra goes on to explain how to live in the world and achieve the supreme goal. The previous mantra had encouraged us to develop spiritual consciousness characterized by thoughts, such as, 'God is the owner and enjoyer of this entire world. All I have belongs to the Lord, and I must use it in His service.' This mantra now reassures us that work performed with the spiritual mindset, for the pleasure of God, will not result in karmic bondage. Why is this so? Consider the following example.

In India, if someone deliberately kills another, he is culpable for the crime of homicide. As per the law, such a person could be sentenced to death. However, when one man has killed another, he is brought to court. The judge questions, 'You killed him?'

'Yes, your honour, I did,' responds the convict.

---

10 'Complete Works of Swami Vivekananda, Vol. IV, The Education that India Needs', *Essential Books of Ramakrishna Order*, https://englishbooks.rkmm.org/s/tsv/m/the-complete-works-of-swami-vivekananda/a/4-5-6-the-education-that-india-needs-1. Last accessed on 15 March 2025.

'Then you must be punished!'

'No, your honour. You cannot punish me. It was not my fault. I was driving the car on the proper side of the road, at the proper speed, with my feet on the brake and hands on the steering. That drunk man suddenly came and fell in front of my car. What could I do?'

If his statement is verified, this person will not receive even the slightest punishment because there was no intention to kill, nor any carelessness.

When work is done with selfish intent, karmic reactions must be borne, as per the Law of Karma. For example, if we do business with the idea of getting wealth for our pleasure, then we will be culpable for any sins committed in our work. However, if we have no attachment to the fruits—and we offer them to God—then it becomes a special category of work, called ***akarm,*** which means **'being the non-doer, even while doing'**. To an onlooker, we may appear to be working, but from a spiritual perspective, we are considered 'non-doers'.

The Bhagavad Gita explains this concept:

yasya nāhankṛito bhāvo buddhir yasya na lipyate
hatvā 'pi sa imāñl lokān na hanti na nibadhyate (18.17)

'Those who are free from the ego of being the doer and whose intellect is unattached, though they may slay living beings, they neither kill nor are they bound by actions.'

The *Ishopanishad* mantra declares the same: *na karma lipyate nare*, meaning 'Work done for the pleasure of God will not result in karmic bondage.' The mantra adds another very profound wisdom here. It says: *aevam tvayi nānyatheto 'sti,* meaning **'there is no simpler means for getting rid of the bonds of karma'**.

Shree Krishna elucidated the same idea to Arjun. Looking on his duties as troublesome, Arjun wanted to renounce them. Shree Krishna, however, explained to him that prematurely renouncing one's works will not meet with success. The nature of the body, mind, and intellect is to remain active. If we leave them idle, they will create trouble and not permit us to be in peace. 'Nobody in this world can remain without action for even a moment. Indeed, all beings are compelled to act by their qualities born of material nature (the three gunas).' (Bhagavad Gita 3.5)

When people develop a spiritual goal, they sometimes make this mistake. They renounce their worldly duties—considering them to be material—and hurry to take sanyas. But without the inner equanimity, they do not progress towards their spiritual goal. Though outwardly renounced, their mind contemplates upon the objects of the senses.

Therefore, one should not rush into taking the step of external renunciation as it can have adverse consequences. Instead, the recommended path is to continue with one's works, while cultivating inner dispassion. A boat stays in the water, but the water does not stay in the boat. Likewise, we should live in the world and continue doing our duties, but not let the world live in us. We must therefore do all our works for His pleasure.

As the mind gets absorbed in the Supreme, the consciousness will get elevated. And then one day the higher stage will be reached where we can renounce all works and simply engage in loving devotion to the Lord.

For the Scholars

Let us briefly understand the three categories of activities: *karm, vikarm,* and *akarm.*

Karm refers to actions we perform in accordance with the varnashram dharma of the scriptures. This is also called karm dharma. It includes our worldly duties and ritualistic ceremonies, such as yajnas.

Karm bestows material prosperity and attainment of the celestial abodes. But the supreme goal of the soul—which is God-realization—is not achieved. Therefore, though the Vedas prescribe karm for regulating human life, they also condemn it. The *Mundakopanishad* states:

iṣhṭāpūrtam manyamānā variṣhṭham
nānyachchhreyo vedayante pramūḍhāḥ
nākasya pṛiṣhṭhe te sukṛite'nubhūtvemam
lokam hīnataram vā viśhanti (1.2.10)

'Foolish people, ignoring acts of eternal welfare, perform Vedic rituals to fulfill material desires. Owing to the fruits of karm-kand, they ascend to the celestial abodes to enjoy the celestial pleasures. However, when their pious merits are depleted, they are reborn on the earth in lower forms of life.'

Vikarm literally means 'opposite of karm'. It refers to prohibited actions, such as stealing others' property, consuming alcohol, gambling, and so on. Another name for *vikarm* is 'sin' or 'impious deeds'.

Likewise, karm can be called 'good deeds'. *Vikarm* results in hell while karm bestows heaven. The *Prashnaopanishad* states:

puṇyena punyam lokam nayati, paapena paapam,
ubhābhyāmeva manuṣhyalokam (Prashna 3, mantra 7)

'If you do good deeds, you will be promoted to the celestial realms. If you do bad deeds, you will be demoted to the nether regions. By doing both good and bad, you will return to the earth realm.'

It is evident that the goal of life is not achieved either through karm or *vikarm*. Now comes the third principle that will result in God-realization.

Akarm. In it, you perform your bodily duties while keeping the mind in God. Since your mind does not hanker for the fruits of the actions, you do not get entangled in karmic reactions. This has been explained in the commentary above.

Karm yog is another name for *akarm*. It will be discussed in detail in mantra 14.

If we do not maintain the spirit of akarm while performing actions, and instead actively hanker for sensual pleasures, then our works become sinful. Subsequently, after death, we will face the consequences of our impious deeds, which are described in the next mantra.

Mantra 3

असुर्या नाम ते लोका अन्धेन तमसाऽऽवृताः ।
तांस्ते प्रेत्याभिगच्छन्ति ये के चात्महनो जनाः ॥ ३॥

asuryā nāma te lokā andhena tamasā ' 'vṛitāḥ
tāṁste pretyābhigachchhanti ye ke chātmahano janāḥ

asuryāḥ—demonic; *nāma*—name; *te*—these; *lokāḥ*—realms; *andhena*—darkness; *tamasā*—of ignorance; *āvṛitāḥ*—covered; *tān*—these realms; *te*—they; *pretya*—after death; *abhigachchhanti*—sent to; *ye*—those; *ke*—everyone; *cha*—and; *ātma-hanaḥ*—squanderers of the soul energy; *janāḥ*—persons.

There are realms without sunshine that are awash with the demonic mindset. They remain covered with the darkness of ignorance that gives sorrow. Humans who expend their soul energy in merely relishing sensual pleasure are sent there after death.

Those in material consciousness are unaware that God is the Proprietor of the world. In ignorance, they identify themselves with the body endowed with five senses. Thus, they pursue sensual gratification with the expectation of finding happiness.

Unfortunately, hedonistic delights only provide momentary excitement, and then, the desire returns. This can be compared to running on a treadmill. One can jog on it for an hour, and yet, physically one remains in the same place. Likewise, even after a lifetime of attempting to fulfill the desires of the senses, one is no happier than before. The Shreemad Bhagavatam explains:

yatpṛithivyām vrīhiyavam hiraṇyam paśhavaḥ striyaḥ
na duhayanti manaḥprītim pumsaḥ kāmahatasya te

(verse 9.19.13)

'All the world's luxuries, gold, women, and opulences will not suffice to satiate the mind of a man who is afflicted by lust.'

If we repeatedly strive to quench a desire, it grows into a craving. And if the craving is for a pleasure that is viewed by society as immoral, it gets labelled as an 'addiction'. The state of craving becomes an 'addiction' when it increases to the point that one loses control over oneself. Addictions grip people so strongly that they ignore even extreme harm to indulge in them.

The etymology of the word 'addiction' in Latin implies 'enslaved by'. If you have ever tried to help people with an addiction, or suffered from one yourself, you will understand why 'enslaved by' is so apt. Hence, the saying that the best time to get rid of an addiction is before it begins.

Under the sway of addictions, desire, and anger, people often cross the line of morality and commit grossly sinful deeds. As a result, the soul suffers a downfall, and in its next life, it is sent to the hellish abodes. The mantra says the fruit of grossly sinful activities is *asūryā*.

Asūryā. The word *sūrya* means 'sun' and *asūryā* means 'without sunlight'. There are regions in the universe that lack illumination from sun-like celestial bodies. Residents of these abodes depend upon fire for the creation of light. The implication is that those who indulge in grossly sinful activities go to the lower worlds.

There is a second meaning to the verse. *Sūrya* is also the biggest source of light, and 'light' is a universal symbol of 'knowledge'. Hence, *asūryā* also means 'without the light of knowledge'. From this perspective, the mantra means 'fruit of sinful activities is birth in regions steeped in ignorance'. These could even be regions on the earth planet itself.

Tamasāvṛitāḥ means 'covered with tamas'. It conveys three special meanings:

1) Tamas could mean 'darkness' from lack of sunlight, as in the case of the nether worlds.
2) Tamas could mean tamo guna, the mode of ignorance, which is the cause of demonic tendencies.
3) Tamas could imply 'ignorance', which is the root cause of bondage of the soul in maya.

Thus, the verse has effectively expressed that those who go to the *asūryā lokas* will be covered by tamas in three ways.

Atma hanaḥ. This word is misinterpreted by scholars to mean *atmahatyā* i.e. 'suicide'. The meaning they ascribe is the attainment of hell after suicide. However, there is again a deeper meaning.

Those who expend their atma-shakti in sensual pleasures cause the downfall of their atma into lower births. This is tantamount to the 'killing of their soul' or *atma hanaḥ*. The *Ramcharitmanas*, using this word, states:

jo na tarai bhava sāgara nara samāja asa pāi
so kṛita nindaka mandamati ātmāhana gati jāi

(*Uttara Kand* 7.44)

'Some do not utilize the human form to cross over the material ocean. Such persons are unintelligent, worthy of reproach, and **killers of their soul**.'

It is true that suicide is a grave sin, and its result is also very torturous. This mantra, however, does not point to the sin of suicide, but to using one's atma-shakti for the pursuit of sinful pleasures resulting in downfall to a lower realm.

Pretya. Some scholars interpret *pretya* as 'attaining the body of a malevolent spirit' owing to unfulfilled desires during one's human life. Keeping this in mind, they understand this mantra as describing the sorrows of existence as a malevolent spirit.

Other scholars interpret *atma hanaḥ* in the mantra to mean suicide. Since the fruit of suicide is that one gets punished to become a disembodied being for a certain period of time, they interpret the word *pretya* in this context.

However, a more suitable meaning of *pretya* is 'after death'. We are being forewarned about sorrows that await us in the afterlife. Thus, the word *pretya* urges us to be careful while we are still alive.

One may wonder about the punishment that awaits the sinful soul in the nether regions. The hellish abodes find mention at numerous places in the Vedic texts. In particular, the *Garud Puran*, the *Agni Puran*, the Shreemad Bhagavatam, and the *Manu Smriti* have elaborate descriptions of hell. While one source describes 28 kinds of hells, another details 21, and yet another claims 7.

In this matter, the *Garud Puran* is considered the most authoritative. It describes 36 kinds of hell where different kinds of punishment are meted out per the impious deeds performed. Just as a sample, a few of the various kinds of hell are described here:

- The killer of cows goes to *Mahāvīchi Narak,* where one is immersed in rotting blood and pricked with thorns.
- Usurpers of others' homes and lands are sent to *Kumbhīpāk Narak,* where they are made to lie on hot sand with burning

fire all around.

- Those who give false testimony are sent to *Raurav Narak*, where they are pierced by hot iron rods.
- Those who enslave innocent people go to *Manjūṣha Narak*, where they are made to lie on a bed with hot iron nails.
- Those who ruin others' married life through false tales and gossip go to *Mahāprabh Narak*, where the entire body is pierced by arrows and whipped.

The description of punishments in these realms is indeed vivid and strikes fear even in the most courageous. It makes people wonder how they can save themselves from hellish destinations. To dissolve this worry, the Bhagavad Gita guides us to avoid three things:

tri-vidham narakasyedam dvāram nāśhanam ātmanaḥ
kāmaḥ krodhas tathā lobhas tasmād etat trayaṁ tyajet

(verse 16.21)

'There are three gates leading to the hell of self-destruction for the soul—desire, anger, and greed. Therefore, one should abandon all three.'

In this verse, Shree Krishna shows the way to avoid the downfall of the soul. He asks us to shun desire, anger, and greed. Instead, we should cultivate virtues, such as self-control, peacefulness, and contentment, which are the true adornments of the soul.

For the Scholars

There is yet another insightful interpretation of this verse. The word *asūryā* also connotes 'asura'. One meaning of *asura* is 'demon'. The straightforward implication then is that those who indulge in sin go to the abodes of the demoniac.

However, from the spiritual perspective, the word *asura* has a deeper meaning. *Asuṣhu ramante iti asurāḥ* 'Asuras are those who rejoice in ephemeral worldly thrills.'

In his bhashya, Shankaracharya interprets asura along the same lines. He writes: *asuryāḥ paramātmabhāvamadvayamapekṣhya devādayo 'pyasurāsteṣhāñcha svabhūtā lokā asuryā nāma* 'Those who lack the divine consciousness of Paramatma are all *asuras,* though they may be celestial gods. And their wealth and abodes are all *asūryā.*'

From this definition, all celestials, humans, and demons who are expending their life energies in the pursuit of worldly pleasures are *asura.* After death, they will come back in the realm of maya, which can be compared to darkness.

This mantra helped crystallize our decision to stay clear of sinful enjoyment. The Upanishad now wants us to cultivate devotion to the Supreme Divine Personality. With this aim, the next mantra introduces us to some of God's astonishing divine attributes and His transcendental nature.

Mantra 4

अनेजदेकं मनसो जवीयो नैनद्देवा आप्नुवन्पूर्वमर्षत् ।
तद्धावतोऽन्यानत्येति तिष्ठत्तस्मिन्नपो मातरिश्वा दधाति ॥ ४॥

anejadekam manaso javīyo
nainaddevā āpnuvanpūrvamarṣhat
taddhāvato 'nyānatyeti tiṣhṭhat
tasminnapo mātariśhvā dadhāti

anejat—unmoved; *ekam*—one; *manasaḥ*—than the mind; *javīyaḥ*—quicker; *na*—not; *enat*—Supreme Divine Personality; *devāḥ*—the celestial gods; *āpnuvan*—approach; *pūrvam*—precedes; *arṣhat*—moves quickly; *tat*—he; *dhāvataḥ*—those who are moving; *anyān*—others; *atyeti*—surpasses; *tiṣhṭhat*—stays still; *tasmin*—in him; *apaḥ*—nurture; *mātariśhvā*—child nurtured in the mother's womb; *dadhāti*—fulfill.

The Supreme Divine Personality, despite remaining unmoved, is quicker than the mind. He alone precedes everything and knows everything. Yet, He cannot be known even by celestial gods. Though He stays still, He surpasses all those who move. This world is like a child nurtured in the womb of God and is fulfilling its purpose.

This mantra gives us a glimpse into the transcendent supra-excellence of God. We are introduced to some of His most astonishing qualities. Though the attributes of the Supreme are inconceivable and immeasurable, nevertheless, the mantra uses powerful literary expressions to convey them.

It starts by saying: 'God is unmoved, and yet He moves quicker than the mind.' Let us understand both these aspects of His personality. ***Anejat*** implies God is '**without movement**'. As per the Sanskrit phrase *aejṛi kampane*, the root *aej* means 'shaking' or 'movement'.

There are two ways in which shaking becomes possible—either by falling from one's state or by changing one's place. However, God cannot fall because His infinite glory is inseparable from Him. This is also why He is known as *achyut*, meaning 'the Infallible One'.

Shaking could also be due to a change of place. This does not happen for the Supreme, simply because He has no need for it. God resides in three distinct ways: 1) He is *lokastha* i.e. 'resides in His abode', 2) *Viśhvastha* 'resides in the entirety of creation', and 3) *Jīvastha*, meaning 'resides in all embodied beings'. Consider these individually.

God is *lokastha*, meaning **'resides in His abode'**. The all-powerful Supreme Lord always lives in His divine abode. The *Brahma Samhita* states:

golokanāmni nijadhāmni tale cha tasya
devi maheśhaharidhāmasu teṣhu teṣhu
te te prabhāvanichayā vihitāśh cha yena
govindamādipuruṣhamtam aham bhājāmi (5.43)

Shree Brahma says, 'In the divine realm, Lord Krishna has an eternal abode called *Golok*. In this divine realm, the eternal abodes of Narayan, Shiv, Durga and other forms of God also exist. I worship that Supreme Personality Shree Krishna by Whose opulence all this has manifest.'

We may ponder how, while living in His abode, can God manage activities related to creation. Vachaspati Mishra explains:

smitametasya charācharamasya cha suptam
mahāpramayaḥ (*Bhamati Teeka*)

'God possesses such powers that when He smiles, the universe gets created, and when He goes to sleep, dissolution happens.' Thus, managing the entirety of creation does not require God to leave His divine abode. He remains unmoved, or is *anejat*.

Again, when God descends in the material realm, He does not renounce His abode. Alongside with His works as an avatar, He simultaneously continues to live in the supreme abode. From this perspective as well, He is *anejat*, or without movement.

God is *viśhvastha*, meaning **'resides in all creation'.** Having made the material realms, the Supreme becomes *viśhvastha*, 'situated in the entire world' to nourish and maintain all beings. The *Maharamayan* states: *bharaṇaḥ poṣhaṇādhāraḥ śharaṇyaḥ sarvavyāpakaḥ* 'The refuge of all entities, that Supreme Lord, has become all-pervading to nourish everyone.'

Not only does God live in all things, but all things also live in Him. Shree Krishna states: 'Everything rests in Me, as beads strung on a thread.' (Bhagavad Gita 7.7)

A good way of understanding this is through the analogy of the sky. It is unaffected by clouds floating in it. Similarly, countless worlds with all their variegated phenomena occur within God, yet He continues to support them while remaining unaffected. The Bhagavad Gita explains:

yathākāśha-sthito nityam vāyuḥ sarvatra-go mahān
tathā sarvāṇi bhūtāni mat-sthānītyupadhāraya (9.6)

'Know that as the mighty wind blows everywhere, and yet always remains in the sky, likewise all living beings always rest in Me.'

Thus, it becomes clear that for the management of creation,

God doesn't need to vibrate, dissipate, or move; He remains *anejat*, or 'unmoved'.

God is *jīvastha*, meaning **'resides in the jivas'**. To track the karmas of all living beings by residing in their heart, does God have to divide and displace Himself? This curiosity is addressed in a very simple way.

Consider the example of the noonday sun that is in a single place but is simultaneously reflected in thousands of lakes on the earth. Similarly, to reside in the hearts of all living entities, God does not need to divide Himself. Though dwelling in all, the Lord's unity of personality remains intact. Thus, though *jīvastha*, God is also *anejat*, meaning 'static' and 'without division'. The *Yogshikha Upanishad* states:

sarvajñam sarvagam śhāntam sarveṣhām hṛidaye sthitam

(verse 3.20)

'That all-knowing, all-pervading, and ever-silent Supreme Lord lives in the heart of all living entities.'

In this manner it has been established beyond doubt that God remains unmoved in His transcendental nature. This is why He is considered *achyut*, or free of changes across forms, places, time, and situations.

Now stating the very reverse, **the mantra describes God as *manaso javīyo*, meaning 'faster than the mind'.** The speed of the mind can be measured in two ways: first is the speed of thought, and second is the speed of change of place. There is a popular saying: *kṣhaṇam yāti pātālam kṣhaṇam yāti nābhasthalam* 'In a moment, the mind reaches the nether regions; and in the next moment, it soars high into the sky.'

Yet, the mind is still no match for the speed of God and cannot travel faster than Him because wherever it goes, God is already present. A fish can swim as fast as possible, but wherever it reaches, the ocean is present from before. Therefore, the speed of our thought can never compare with God's speed.

On examining the mind's power of contemplation, we find it has a restricted periphery. Our material mind is not capable of contemplating the divine realm. The *Ramcharitmanas* states:

go gochar jahaṅ lagi mana jāī, so saba māyā jānehu bhāī

(*Aranya Kand* 3.14.2)

'Wherever the mind can go is all the realm of maya.' Thus, our mind can contemplate only the material world, and even that, to a limited extent.

God, on the other hand, is the Supreme Controller of both the divine and the material worlds. Thus, the capabilities of mind are bested by God. He is, hence, known as *manaso javīyo*, 'the One Who is faster than the mind'.

From this we can conclude that **the Supreme cannot be known by the mind and intellect.** At this point, one may wonder that while ordinary humans cannot know God, perhaps residents of celestial realms—with their vastly superior intellect—can know him. This curiosity is resolved by the mantra: *na aenat devāḥ* 'Not even the devatas can know God.'

The reason is explained in two ways. First, God is *pūrvam* i.e. He is 'the One Who came before everyone else'. The celestial gods were manifest from His infinite potency, so they came after Him.

Second, God is *arṣhat*, meaning 'the One Who illumines'.

The senses, mind, and intellect of all living beings receive their power to work from God. Even the potencies of celestial beings come from Him. This insight shines through in a very interesting story from the *Kenopanishad*.

Once, at the end of a war with the asuras, the devatas sat gloating, thinking they had won solely because of their strength. God did not appreciate their arrogance and promptly enacted a leela to shatter their pride.

In the celestial sky, the Supreme appeared as an effulgent light. Wondering what the luminous object was, Indra sent Agni for investigation. God put a blade of grass in front of Agni and asked him to burn it. But as Agni moved forward to perform the task, the Lord withdrew the potency of heat from him. Alas, not only did Agni fail to burn the blade of grass, but he also became cold himself! Embarrassed and defeated, Agni returned to Indra's council.

Subsequently, Vayu was sent to investigate, and the Lord asked him to move the same blade of grass. Approaching it with tremendous speed, Vayu also failed and became static. Situated in Vayu's heart, God had suppressed Vayu's powers. Defeated and his pride destroyed, Vayu returned to Indra's assembly.

Worried, now Indra himself came to investigate the light. God however disappeared, and Yogmaya sat in His place. She scolded Indra, 'Your eternal Father had come to destroy your pride. After winning the battle against the asuras, you had forgotten that the source of your power was God. Of all the celestials, your vanity knew no bounds. Thus, God decided not to meet you or even speak to you.' Humbled and filled with repentance, Indra returned, contemplating God's glories.

The story highlights that even celestial personalities with vast potencies are nothing without the power of the Supreme.

Further, narrating God's inconceivable glory, the mantra says: *tat anyān dhāvataḥ tiṣhṭhat atyeti* i.e. **'while remaining stationary, God bests all those who run'**. In all of creation, whatever moves gets its power from God, Who always remains beyond and unaffected.

Mātariśhvā. This word has many meanings, prominent amongst which is 'Vayu'. Earlier, we saw that all devatas operate by the power of God. Then why is Vayu being singled out for repetition? Thus, we cannot take *mātariśhvā* to mean 'vayu' or 'prana'.

There is a deeper meaning: *mātri antarīkṣhe svayati iti mātriśhvan* i.e. 'that which grows within the space of the mother's womb'. An unborn baby develops in the mother's womb, where it is nourished.

Similarly, this world is sustained by God and derives support from Him for its functioning. Hence, we can regard the world as *mātariśhvā*. It is nurtured in the womb of God, and it is fulfilling the purpose for which it was created. This purpose was discussed in the explanation to the *Shanti Path Mantra.*

We have understood that the Supreme Divine Personality is the foundation of all things that exist. To heighten our devotion towards Him, this mantra gave us a brief introduction to His transcendent excellence. In the next mantra, His attributes are further elaborated. Let us learn how He uses His inconceivable potencies to manifest contradictory attributes and also support them.

Mantra 5

तदेजति तन्नैजति तद्दूरे तद्वन्तिके ।
तदन्तरस्य सर्वस्य तदु सर्वस्यास्य बाह्यतः ॥ ५॥

tadejati tannaijati taddūre tadvantike
tadantarasya sarvasya tadu sarvasyāsya bāhyataḥ

tat—that Supreme Lord; *aejati*—walks; *tat*—he; *na*—not; *aejati*—walks; *tat*—he; *dūre*—farther away; *tat*—he; *u*—also; *antike*—very close; *tat*—he; *antaḥ*—within; *asya*—of this; *sarvasya*—everything; *tat*—he; *u*—also; *sarvasya*—everything; *asya*—of this; *bāhyataḥ*—outside.

That Supreme Lord walks, while remaining still. He is very far and also extremely close. Though He resides within everything in this world, yet He is also present outside this creation.

The Creator Who made the dualities—light and darkness, heat and cold, pleasure and pain—possesses conflicting attributes within Himself as well. Here are some astonishing ones.

God walks, while remaining still. In fact, the world too has a dual static-moving nature. In Sanskrit, 'world' is called *sansar*. It is defined as: *sansaratīti sansārah*, meaning 'the world is that which is always slipping away'.

This slipping happens in many ways. The ancient Greek philosopher, Heraclitus,[11] had brilliantly explained that no man

[11] 'Heraclitus', Stanford Encyclopedia of Philosophy, 3.1 Flux, https://plato.

ever steps in the same river twice, for it's not the same river and he's not the same man. The next time you step into the river, you have changed and so has the river. Similarly, objects may appear the same to us, but they are actually changing. A mango we plucked from a tree begins to rot in a couple of days. Trees themselves undergo change every day as they shed leaves and grow new ones.

Our life too keeps moving from year to year. The cells in our body regenerate, while the body transforms from childhood to youth to old age. Our emotions, wisdom, and memories continuously shift. The option of returning to the past is never available—you can only move forward, whether you like it or not.

It is thus established that the world keeps shifting in every way. Now, connect this with the fact that the world is *viśhvarūpa* (cosmic form of the Lord). It means when the world moves, God moves alongside. Hence, one implication of *tadejati* is 'God moves in the form of the world'.

Yet, even while moving, He remains the unmoving foundation of the world. For instance, noon-time travellers in a desert find that the sun appears to move with them. In fact, however, the sun remains positioned at the centre of the solar system. Similarly, there is no question of God's movement. He is all-pervading and everywhere at all times. On His unshakeable foundation, the sansar continues to slip. From this perspective, the mantra says *tannaijati*, meaning **'God is static'**.

Let us now consider God's movement with respect to the

---

stanford.edu/entries/heraclitus/#Flu. Last accessed on 10 January 2025.

individual souls. As Paramatma, He is situated in the heart of all living beings. The *Shwetashvatar Upanishad* states: *chetanaśhchetanānām aeko bahūnām* (6.13) 'The Lord resides within countless souls, enlivening them.' Therefore, He accompanies us as we transmigrate from life to life. From this perspective, *tadejati* means **'God moves with the souls'**.

But the reverse is also true. He is the innermost witness who tracks our karmas and bestows the fruits of our actions. Yet, He is unaffected by the travails that engulf the living being. Hence, *tat na aejati* i.e. **'God remains static' as the untouched basis of our life.**

Third, let us examine this mantra from the perspective of devotional sentiments. On one hand, God is the dispenser of justice through the Law of Karma. He maintains order in creation without partiality. Then what explains the variations we see in the world?

Compare this to rain. The rainwater falls equally upon the earth. Yet, the drop that falls on the cornfields gets converted into grain. The drop that falls near a desert bush gets transformed into a thorn. The drop that falls in the gutter becomes dirty water. And the drop that falls in the oyster becomes a pearl. There is no partiality on behalf of the rain—the variation observed is because of the nature of the recipients.

Similarly, the Lord says in the Bhagavad Gita:

samo 'ham sarva-bhūteṣhu na me dveṣhyo 'sti na priyaḥ

(verse 9.29)

'I am equally disposed to all living beings; I am neither inimical nor partial to anyone.' From this perspective, *tat na aejati* i.e. **'God is unmoved', being equal to all.**

On the other hand, the second line of the above verse of the Bhagavad Gita states:

ye bhajanti tu mām bhaktyā mayi te teṣhu chāpyaham

(verse 9.29)

'But the devotees who worship Me with love reside in Me, and I reside in them.'

Upon His devotees, the Lord bestows His special graces—divine knowledge, divine bliss, and divine love, so much so that He even becomes enslaved by selfless devotion. Under its sway, He performs sweet pastimes with His devotees. For example, while the souls of the world remain bound in Shree Krishna's maya shakti, He permits Himself to be tied to a grinding wheel by Mother Yashoda because of her maternal love for Him. From this perspective, *tat aejati* means **devotion makes His heart melt, and God moves.**

Next, the mantra states another set of contradictory attributes of the Lord. It says: God is far, yet He is also near; *taddūre tadvantike*. Let us look at these individually.

God is far, *taddūre*. He is so far that He is beyond the entire material cosmos.

God is near, *tadvantike*. He is so near to us that even the word 'near' is inappropriate since He resides within us as the indwelling Paramatma.

This contrariness can be investigated from the devotional perspective as well. In the absence of faith, love, and surrender

God remains unreachable. Those who are proud of their sadhana end up going further away. But the same Lord responds immediately when a surrendered soul calls out to Him with loving devotion. The *Narad Bhakti Darshan* explains:

īśhvarasyāpyabhimāndveṣhitvāt dainyapriyatvāt cha

(sutra 27)

'God hates pride in the heart of devotees, while He loves humility.' In this way, for the arrogant, the Supreme is far. Yet for the humble devotees, He is close and responds immediately. A popular Hindi idiom reveals how God reciprocates with the jiva:

jo tū dhāve aeka paga to main dhāūn sāṭha
jo tū karro kāṭh to main lohe kī lāṭh

'If you take one step towards Me with love, I will run 60 steps towards you. But if you are stubborn and disobey My instructions, I will punish you severely.'

Continuing with the description of God's contrary virtues, the mantra states:

He resides within everything, *tadantarasya sarvasya.* The first mantra of the Upanishad had declared that God is all-pervading, which implies that every speck of creation has His presence.

He is outside the entire world, *tadu sarvasyāsya bāhyataḥ.* All creation exists within the Supreme. Also, at the time of dissolution of creation, God absorbs it back into Himself. This confirms that He is outside the world.

Thus, God resides everywhere, both within the world and outside it. The Puranas confirm this insight with a very interesting tale.

Once Devarshi Narad obtained a very beautiful fruit and felt inspired to offer it to Bhagavan Shiv. Upon reaching Shankarji's abode, Kailash, he offered the juicy fruit to Him. Both the sons of Shiv, Ganesh and Kartikeya, saw the fruit and started arguing that it be given to them. To resolve the matter, Shiv announced a competition. Whoever would circumambulate the universe and come to Him first would obtain the fruit. The celestial sage Narad stayed on to find out who would win.

The valiant Kartikeya mounted his peacock and left immediately to complete the circumambulation of the entire universe. Ganesh found himself disadvantaged with his plump body, so instead, he hit upon a brilliant idea. He got Gauri Shankar to sit on a stone platform, did Their parikrama thrice, and asked his Father for the fruit. Lord Shiv replied, 'Son, you have only walked around us thrice, while your brother has already left at great speed to cover the universe.'

Ganesh responded, 'Father, since you are God, the entire creation resides within You. Thus, I have circumambulated the entire universe thrice.' Hearing this deep insight, Shiv and Parvati burst into laughter and could not disagree with Ganesh. When Kartikeya returned, he found Ganesh had already eaten the fruit.

The story brings forth the philosophic insight that God is both inside and outside the world. A similar pastime was enacted by Shree Krishna as well. When Mother Yashoda made Him open His mouth, the Lord showed her innumerable universes within it, including her and Krishna.

Yogmaya—God's all-powerful shakti. What is God's secret ability that enables Him to do this? It is His Yogmaya power, which is His internal potency. The Lord is the Master of Yogmaya. This all-powerful shakti of God enables Him to be *kartumakartum anyathā kartum samarthaḥ* 'Possessing the ability to do what is possible, what is impossible, and what is mutually converse.'

Just as God takes on various personal forms, such as Narayan, Krishna, Ram, and Shiv, similarly, the Yogmaya shakti also manifests in the personal form as Lakshmi, Radha, Sita, and Parvati. These forms of the Yogmaya power are revered in the world by the name 'Mother of the universe'.

Towards the all-powerful God, we must cultivate our devotion, by appreciating Him as the foundation of all creation and the Possessor of infinite divine virtues. We must practise perceiving His presence everywhere in the world. The changes that will take place in our consciousness as a result of doing so are described in the next mantra.

Mantra 6

यस्तु सर्वाणि भूतान्यात्मन्येवानुपश्यति ।
सर्वभूतेषु चात्मानं ततो न विजुगुप्सते ॥ ६॥

yastu sarvāṇi bhūtānyātmanyevānupaśhyati
sarvabhūteṣhu chātmānam tato na vijugupsate

yaḥ—those who; *tu*—but; *sarvāṇi*—all; *bhūtāni*—living beings; *ātmani*—in relation to God; *eva*—only; *anupaśhyati*—perceives; *sarva-bhūteṣhu*—in all living being; *cha*—and; *ātmānam*—the

Supreme Soul; *tataḥ*—thereafter; *na*—not; *vijugupsate*—hates anyone.

All living beings are situated in God, and He resides in all living beings. One who clearly perceives this Truth does not hate anyone.

When spiritual aspirants start perceiving God everywhere—as the origin and basis of creation—their sight, emotions, and actions undergo a transformation. This mantra describes how these changes are reflected in our thoughts, sentiments, and behaviour.

Jugupsā. The word is constructed from root words *gup* and *san*. It implies thought waves of bitterness or hatred. *Vijugupsā* means an enhanced form of these negative sentiments. From a philosophical perspective, *vijugupsā* encompasses two kinds of lower thought forms.

1) **Hatred.** We resent others when they interfere with the fulfillment of our desires. We contemplate the person's faults and become averse with bitterness. This is the aspect of hatred or deep aversion in *vijugupsā*.

2) **Envy.** It means harbouring bitterness towards others due to their virtues or triumphs. Why does this negative emotion arise? On seeing others' accomplishments, we become painfully aware of our own failures and shortcomings. As a result, we harbour resentment towards them. The negativity subsequently takes the form of condemnation and criticism. This is the jealousy aspect of *vijugupsā*.

Vijugupsā causes us to commit violence by our thoughts, words, and deeds. Instead of harbouring such negativity, we should approach others with respect and admiration, since they are living examples of the human potential for progress. Besides, ultimately all talents come from God. So, envy of others' abilities is, in effect, envy of God Himself.

The question arises: How can we get rid of hatred and envy? The solution, the mantra provides, is to learn to see God situated in everyone.

Anupaśhyati. In Sanskrit, *paśhyati* has two meanings: 1) to see with the eyes, and 2) to see as per spiritual knowledge. By the second definition, *anupaśhyati* means 'to see clearly as per spiritual knowledge'.

Spiritual books are called Darshan Shastras, meaning 'books that enable us to see'. This phrase has a very deep import. Usually, we do not realize the biases in the way we see things.

A professor once showed his students a blank paper with a big dot in the centre. He asked them what they saw. Without exception, they all responded that they saw the black dot. The professor then pointed out that manifold more than the dot was the empty space around it. But they had failed to see it because they had only focused on the prominent object.

Likewise, we assume the way we see the world is exactly how it is—we do not realize how tainted our perspective is. Chanakya Pandit states:

noluko 'pyavalokate yadi diva sūryasya kim dūṣhaṇam

(*Chanakya Neeti* 12.5)

'If the owl is unable to see during the day, it is not the fault of the sun.'

Similarly, God is present everywhere in this world, but we fail to see Him. This is not a defect in the world but in our vision. The Darshan Shastras teach us to truly see things in proper light. This is *śhāstra chakṣhu,* meaning 'to see through the eyes of the scriptures'. It is also called *jñana chakṣhu*, meaning 'to see through the eyes of knowledge'.

The mantra asks us to cultivate the vision that the Lord resides in all. This instruction is not merely a flight of fancy. The Vedas inform us that the world is in fact the veritable form of God. The *Mundakopanishad* teaches that God Himself becomes the world:

yathorṇanābhiḥ sṛijate gṛihṇate cha
yathā pṛithivyāmoṣhadhayaḥ sambhavanti
yathā sataḥ puruṣhāt keśhalomāni
tathā 'kṣharāt sambhavatīha viśhvam (1.1.7)

This verse gives three very powerful analogies to explain that the world is an aspect of the Divine.

1) Spiders spin amazing webs. Astonishingly, spider thread has a tensile strength, per gram weight, that is even higher than steel. To top it, the strands of the web are waterproof. Even scientists are intrigued by this material. It is extracted by the spider from within itself. And when the web is no longer required, the spider sometimes takes it back into itself. Like the spider, God extracts the material energy from within His being at *sṛiṣhṭi* (creation), and then withdraws it back at *pralaya* (dissolution).

2) From the earth, trees spring forth. The mud itself transforms into the trees. Then one day, the tree dies and becomes mud again. Likewise, by unravelling His material energy, God

Himself becomes the world. Then, one day, the world goes back into God.

3) Hair shoot out on humans. These are not planted from the outside. The body itself shoots out in the form of hair. Similarly, the materials that constitute the world are manifested from God Himself.

When we learn to see everything in its connection with the Divine, then it becomes worthy of our worship.

The story is told of a small non-profit organization that was experiencing bitter conflicts amongst its volunteers. Its president went to a guru, and said, 'O Sage! We are unable to get along with each other. This seriously debilitates our functioning, rendering us ineffective as an organization.'

The sage responded, 'The reason is that an avatar of God is in the midst of your volunteers. He works incognito, so you do not recognize Him. But since you all misbehave so much towards Him, it has resulted in great inauspiciousness for the organization.'

The president returned and began thinking who amongst the volunteers could be the avatar. None was free from defects. But then if God was working incognito, He would be hiding Himself behind a veneer of defects. So, the president decided to call a meeting and informed everyone about what the sage had said.

This information that one amongst them was an avatar, changed the volunteers' behaviour towards each other. They stopped quarrelling and became respectful. In a little while the atmosphere became harmonious and the organization became effective.

Along these lines, this mantra encourages us to see God

everywhere. The word *anupaśhyati* in the mantra is telling us to develop the eyes of knowledge. It must be done towards all living beings. So, let us consider the two words used.

Bhūtāni and ***bhūteṣhu.*** These words in the mantra are worthy of special attention. They refer to the multitude of living beings.

The word *bhūta* comes from the root *bhū sattāyām*, which means 'that which is full of life'. Here, it is employed as a plural, *bhūtāni*, referring to 'multiple living beings'. Further, the *adhikaran vibhakti* form, *bhūteṣhu*, is used to refer to 'something common inside all living beings'.

The mantra is thus asking us to develop a twofold vision: 1) to see the presence of God in living beings, and 2) to see all living beings in God's omnipresence.

This grand unity of all living beings with God—when perceived—will dispel the illusion of their independent existence from our intellect. Then, we will develop equanimity of vision. From it, will arise a purified state of mind, described as *na vijugupsate* i.e. 'does not hate or envy anyone'. The Bhagavad Gita states the same principle:

yo mām paśhyati sarvatra sarvam cha mayi paśhyati
tasyāham na praṇaśhyāmi sa cha me na praṇaśhyati

(verse 6.30)

'To those devotees—who perceive Me everywhere in the world and see Me in all living beings—I am never lost to them, nor are they ever lost to Me.'

Therefore, the main means of reducing *vijugupsā* is to feel the

Divine presence everywhere. Then, with equanimity of vision, we will not engage in violence of thought, speech, or actions towards anyone.

For the Scholars

On hearing that God brings forth the raw material of the world from His own Being, some scholars ask a question: 'The Supreme is sentient. How has insentient material energy manifested from Him?'

The answer is, in fact, quite simple. We see the same contradiction within ourselves. Understand from this example, presented in a lighter vein:

Shivdutt was sleeping soundly. Vishnudutt came with a pair of scissors, and cut his choti—tuft of hair at the back of the head. When Shivdutt woke up, he was shocked to discover his choti was gone.

How did Shivdutt not know when his choti was being cut? Had it been stuck on his head from the outside? No, it had grown from his body itself.

Look at the wonder! From the sentient body, the insentient hair grows. While the body has life, the hair does not. Now consider the second scenario.

While Shivdutt was awake, Vishnudutt came from behind and slightly pulled a few hairs on his head. Shivdutt screamed, 'Aah...! My head is paining.'

'But your hair is insentient. Even when it is cut, you do not come to know. Then why is it paining now?'

'Yes, my hair is insentient, but this time you pulled the sentient

portion of the hair. And that is causing the pain.'

Again, look at the wonder! The same hair has a sentient portion and an insentient portion. One segment of the hair carries the sensation of pain, while the other does not. Likewise, there is no contradiction if, from the sentient God, the insentient material energy manifests.

The ideal spiritual practices and recommended behaviour for spiritual aspirants have been explained thus far. In the next mantra, the aspirant's inner state is described when perfection is attained.

Mantra 7

यस्मिन्सर्वाणि भूतान्यात्मैवाभूद्विजानतः ।
तत्र को मोहः कः शोक एकत्वमनुपश्यतः ॥७॥

yasminsarvāṇi bhūtānyātmaivābhūdvijānataḥ
tatra ko mohaḥ kaḥ śhoka ekatvamanupaśhyataḥ

yasmin—in which; *sarvāṇi*—all; *bhūtāni*—living beings; *ātmā*—God; *eva*—only; *abhūt*—exist as; *vijānataḥ*—of one who knows; *tatra*—therein; *kaḥ*—what; *mohaḥ*—delusion; *kaḥ*—what; *śhokaḥ*—grief; *ekatvam*—oneness in quality; *anupaśhyataḥ*—of one who sees like that.

All living beings reside in God, and He resides in all living beings. One who clearly knows this Truth sees the unity of all creation with the Lord. For such a realized sage, how can there be delusion or grief?

This mantra demystifies the sublime consciousness of God-realized souls. In this illumined state, their knowledge, awareness, and experience, all align with the Divine. Let us try to understand how.

In mantra 6, the word *anupaśhyati* was used, meaning 'to see clearly as per spiritual knowledge'. At this stage, the sadhak is in the process of spiritual practice.

In mantra 7, *anupaśhyataḥ* and *vijānataḥ* are used, meaning 'to definitely see' and 'to definitely know' respectively. These words indicate a higher spiritual state. The aspirant has attained perfection of divine vision, and the entire consciousness is now united with God.

The mantra explains that at that stage of divine consciousness, *moha* 'delusion' and *śhoka* 'lamentation' both fall away naturally. To comprehend this necessitates a discussion on delusion and sorrow.

***Moha* (delusion)**. It comes from the root *muh*, meaning 'state of unconsciousness'. Hence, the word *moha* means 'that which causes unconsciousness'. It refers to delusion. One experiences *moha* when one is in delusion.

This *moha* is the root of all problems. The *Ramcharitmanas* states:

> *moha sakala byādhinha kara mūlā*
> *tinha te puni upajahin bahu sūlā*
>
> (*Uttara Kand* 7.120.15)

'*Moha* is the cause of all mental and psychological afflictions. It makes many thorn-like obstacles to appear.' The first of these afflictions is 'clouding of judgement'.

The Bhagavad Gita states the same point: *sammohāt smṛiti-vibhramaḥ. smṛiti-bhranśhād buddhi-nāśho buddhi-nāśhāt praṇaśhyati* (2.63).

'*Moha* results in bewilderment of memory. When memory is bewildered, the intellect gets destroyed; and when the intellect is destroyed, one is ruined.'

Thus, *moha* is the opposite of the intellect's wisdom. With the right knowledge in place, *moha* gets destroyed. Let us learn from this story.

A man found a few pieces of glass and believed them to be diamonds. Owing to the faulty decision of his intellect, he experienced the false joy of owning diamonds.

One day, he went to sell the glass pieces in the marketplace. A diamond merchant, on inspecting them, realized they were not diamonds at all. He dispelled the man's illusion by shattering the glass pieces with a stone.

The moment the man realized the truth, his moha *about being the owner of diamonds was destroyed. Nonetheless, based on them, he had dreamed of a luxurious life. Now that the diamonds were gone, his dream was also shattered, and he wept loudly. His own* moha *had become the reason for his sorrow.*

***Śhoka* (sorrow)**. The above story elucidates that wherever there is *moha*, it is followed by sorrow. These two form an inseparable pair. The same object of our *moha* becomes the reason for our sorrow. As *moha* is opposite of wisdom, so also is sorrow the opposite of it.

To destroy Arjun's worldly sorrow, Shree Krishna spoke the Gita. In fact, the very first verse He spoke to Arjun was:

aśhochyān-anvaśhochas-tvam
prajñā-vādānśh cha bhāṣhase
gatāsūn-agatāsūnśh-cha
nānuśhochanti paṇḍitāḥ (2.11)

'While you speak words of wisdom, you are mourning (doing *śhoka*) for that which is not worthy of sorrow. The wise lament neither for the living nor for the dead.'

At the very end of the Bhagavad Gita, again Shree Krishna addressed Arjun: 'O Arjun! Have your ignorance and *moha* (delusion) been destroyed?' (BG 18.72) *kachchid ajñāna-sammohaḥ pranaṣhṭas te dhanañjaya.*

Responding to this question, Arjun replied: 'O Shree Krishna, by Your grace, my *moha* has been destroyed and the loss of memory has also been rectified. As a result, my spiritual knowledge has returned.' (BG 18.73) *naṣhṭo mohaḥ smṛitir labdhā tvat-prasādān mayāchyuta.*

It is important to note that Shree Krishna only asked Arjun whether he was free from *moha* or not. In his response, Arjun only spoke about the destruction of *moha*. Shree Krishna neither inquired about Arjun's sorrow, nor did Arjun mention anything about it.

The spiritual principle is: *moha* and *śhoka* are a correlated pair. Hence, the destruction of *moha* is also the destruction of sorrow. *Śhoka* occurs when we harbour *moha* towards objects, people, or circumstances, and we lose them or fear losing them.

Arjun was experiencing *moha* towards those he was deeply

attached to. Thus, when his *moha* was destroyed, the *śhoka* on their death was also destroyed. Arjun's reply, therefore, was only about *moha*.

The *Ishopanishad* reconfirms the same insight by saying: 'For those who have perfected divine vision, how can there be delusion? Without delusion, how can there be sorrow? God-realized saints are beyond the twin thorns of delusion and sorrow and are ever joyful.' They remain steadfast and resolute in God's service and engage in the welfare of all living entities.

This mantra provides us a litmus test to know whether we have attained our spiritual goal. If our emotions oscillate between hankering and lamentation, then we do not yet possess divine vision. We must continue our spiritual practice with humility and not pretend to have attained the stage of perfection.

For the Scholars

Some scholars believe that the phrase *aekatvam anupaśhyataḥ* in the mantra points to the philosophy of *Advaita*. Thus, they declare that upon attaining perfection, a jiva loses its individual existence and becomes one with the Formless Absolute. However, we must understand the phrase with reference to the context.

In the previous mantra, by means of *anupaśhyati*, progress in sadhana was conveyed. In this mantra, *anupaśhyataḥ* conveys that the same sadhana has now reached *siddhi,* meaning perfection. Now the *siddha* sees the unity of the entire world with God. This is the *aekatva*, meaning 'oneness of the consciousness with God'.

Sage Narad talks of this oneness of perception in his *Bhakti Darshan*:

tatprāpya tadevāvalokayati, tadeva śhṛiṇoti,
tadeva bhāṣhayati, tadeva chintayati (sutra 55)

'After obtaining this love, one sees Him alone, hears about Him alone, describes Him alone, and thinks of Him alone.'

The Shreemad Bhagavatam also describes this elevated state of consciousness where one sees God everywhere.

sarvabhūteṣhu yaḥ paśhyed bhagavadbhāvamātmanaḥ
bhūtāni bhagavatyātmanyeṣha bhāgavatottamaḥ

(verse 11.2.45)

'Those who see God in all beings and realize that everything is eternally situated in the Supreme, such devotees are the highest of all.'

This experience is fully aligned with the *Vishishta Advaita* of Ramanujacharya, the *Vishuddha Advaita* of Vallabhacharya, the *Achintya Bhedabhed* of Chaitanya Mahaprabhu, and the *Dvaita Advaita* of Nimbarkacharya.

All these great acharyas have talked about the unity of the jiva with God. They have also described that on God-realization, the soul becomes one with God, in the sense that the consciousness gets united. For example, the *Ramcharitmanas* states: *jānata tumhahi tumhai hoi jāī* (*Ayodhya Kand* 2.126.2) 'On knowing God, the soul becomes God-like.' But this does not mean the soul itself becomes God.

The elevated state discussed in this mantra requires dedicated spiritual practice and the cultivation of devotion. The next mantra takes us further in this direction by going even deeper into the qualities and nature of the Supreme Divine Personality.

Mantra 8

स पर्यगाच्छुक्रमकायमव्रण
मस्नाविरं शुद्धमपापविद्धम् ।
कविर्मनीषी परिभूः स्वयम्भूर्याथातथ्यतो
ऽर्थान् व्यदधाच्छाश्वतीभ्यः समाभ्यः ॥ ८॥

sa paryagāchchhukramakāyamavraṇa
masnāviram śhuddhamapaapaviddham
kavirmanīṣhī paribhūḥ svayambhūryāthātathyato
'rthān vyadadhāchchhāśhvatībhyaḥ samābhyaḥ

saḥ—that person; *paryagāt*—attain; *śhukram*—the all-powerful; *akāyam*—without a material body (of veins and blood vessels); *avraṇam*—without wounds, unscathed; *asnāviram*—without veins; *śhuddham*—pure, beyond material defects; *apaapaviddham*—untouched by sin; *kaviḥ*—omniscient; *manīṣhī*—full of wisdom; *paribhūḥ*—omnipresent; *svayambhūḥ*—self-manifest; *yāthātathyataḥ*—in accordance with their karmas; *arthān*—desirable objects; *vyadadhāt*—awards; *śhāśhvatībhyaḥ*—immemorial; *samābhyaḥ*—time.

Such a saintly person truly attains the supremely resplendent and omnipotent God, Who is without a body of veins and blood vessels. His form is beyond material defects and is ever untouched by sin. That Supreme

Personality is all-knowing, full of wisdom, all-pervading, and self-manifest. Since time immemorial, He has been bestowing desirable objects to embodied beings based on their karmas.

The *Ishavasya Upanishad* now delves deeper into the nature of the Supreme Divine Personality. In this mantra, God is described through 11 prominent names. These can be divided into three categories covering different aspects of His personality.

1) *Guna-vāchak* or names that describe God's attributes.

2) *Svarūpa-vāchak* or names related to the nature of His form.

3) *Kriya-vāchak* or names describing His works.

Come, let us take a closer look into these, as it will enhance our appreciation of His glories.

***Guna-vāchak nāma*. These are names describing God's attributes.**

1. *Śhukram.* This name of God implies 'He Who is endowed with the highest extent of brilliance and omnipotence.' This word is used for the Supreme in the *Mundakopanishad* as well.

> *upāsate puruṣham ye hyakāmāḥ te*
> *śhukrametadativartanti dhīrāḥ* (mantra 3.2.1)

'The humble and peaceful ones who selflessly worship the Supreme are victorious over the world. They attain that omnipotent Shukra.'

2. *Śhuddham.* Etymologically, the word *śhuddham* is composed of the roots *śhudha* and *kta*, meaning 'manifesting purity'. As a descriptive for God, *śhuddham* literally means 'The Pure One'.

Defects are a consequence of the material energy, maya. However, just as darkness cannot overwhelm the sun, likewise, maya cannot even come close to the Supreme. Being ever beyond its purview, He is without blemish and free from defects. Therefore, our mind too gets purified by absorbing it in the Lord. As it gets cleansed, the soul perceives more aspects of God's divine attributes.

3. ***Apāpaviddhaḥ.*** It means 'One who remains untouched by pious and impious deeds'.

The Law of Karma applies to us materially bound souls because we work with selfish intent for the sake of our own happiness. As a result, we are obliged to bear the karmic consequences of our actions. Karma, however, does not apply to the Lord because He has no selfish intention whatsoever. The *Taittiriya Upanishad* states: 'Know the Supreme to be the form of Bliss.' (3.6) He has no need for bliss from external sources. Since God is free from self-seeking, He is beyond the Law of Karma.

Confirming this, Shree Krishna says in the Bhagavad Gita:

na mām karmāṇi limpanti na me karma-phale spṛihā

(verse 4.14)

'O Arjun, no karma can bind Me, since I have no desire for the fruit of actions.'

The question is asked by some: 'Shree Krishna stole butter from the homes of the gopis. Isn't that a sin?'

The answer is that whatever Shree Krishna did was for the welfare of the souls. In this particular case, the gopis eagerly yearned for 'Mākhan Chor' *(Butter Thief) to come and steal their butter.*

While extracting it from yogurt, they would think, 'Krishna! Krishna!'

As the Knower of their heart, He fulfilled their wishes. His stealing butter was to give pleasure to His devotees. In the process, He also enacted divine leelas that provided the basis for bhakti to billions of devotees ever since.

The *Ramcharitmanas* uses the splendid analogy of the wind, sun, and fire in this verse:

samaratha kahuñ nahin doṣhu gosāīn
rabi pāvaka sursari kī nāīn (*Bal Kand* 1.68.4)

This verse explains that the all-powerful is unaffected by impurities. It conveys the idea with three vivid analogies: 1) When the sun's rays fall on dirty water, does the sun become impure? Of course not! On the contrary, the water gets purified. 2) Again, wind flows through an impure place, does the wind god become impure? Definitely not! Rather, the place gets cleansed of impurities. 3) Yet again, does the Ganga become an impure river because dirty streams flow into it? Never! Instead, the unclean streams become the Ganga. Likewise, the all-pure God is untouched by sins.

The Shreemad Bhagavatam goes a step further. It explains that even pure-hearted saints are not bound by the fruitive reactions of work.

yatpādapaṅkajaparāganiṣhevatṛiptā
yogaprabhāvavidhutākhilakarmabandhāḥ
svairam charanti munayo 'pi na nahyamānā-
stasyechchhayāttavapuṣhaḥ kuta aeva bandhaḥ

(10.33.35)

'Material activities never taint the devotees of God who are fully satisfied in serving the dust of His lotus feet. Nor do material activities taint those wise sages who have freed themselves from the bondage of karmic reactions by the power of Yog. So where is the question of bondage for the Lord Himself, Who assumes His transcendental form by His own sweet will?'

Meaning of 'Nirgun'. The three *guna vāchak* names of God are proof of His divine attributes. This refutes the jnani's notion that God is *nirgun* (without attributes). In the context of the Supreme, *nirgun* means 'without material gunas (qualities)'. The *Padma Puran* states:

yo 'sau nirguṇa ityuktaḥ śhāstreṣhu jagadīśhvaraḥ
prākṛitair heyasanyuktair guṇair hīrnatvamuchyate

(6.227.40-41)

'When the Lord of the world is said to be nirgun in the scriptures, it implies that He does not have material attributes.' But He possesses innumerable divine attributes.

***Svarūpa-vāchak nāma.* These are names describing God's divine form.**

4. *Akāyam.* This name can be understood with three different perspectives:

i) Being radiant, God's divine form is not visible, and hence, He is *akāya*. This meaning aligns with mantras 15 and 16 of the Upanishad, where the devotee prays to the Lord to reveal His divine form by hiding His effulgence.

ii) As God is covered by Yogmaya, His *kāyā* (form) is not visible to everyone. The Bhagavad Gita states:

nāham prakāśhaḥ sarvasya yoga-māyā-samāvṛitaḥ

(verse 7.25)

Shree Krishna says, 'I am not manifest to everyone, being veiled by My divine Yogmaya energy.'

iii) *Akāya* is 'He in Whom there is no difference between Himself and His body.'

dehadehīvibhedo 'yam neśhvare vidyate kvachit

(*Kurma Puran*)

deha-dehī-bhidā chaiva neśhvare vidyate kvachit

(*Narad Pancharatra*)

Both these verses imply that for the Supreme Divine Personality there is no distinction between the body and the embodied.

Our body houses physical parts, working senses, knowledge senses, mind, intellect, ego, and the atma. All these entities perform specific functions. However, in the case of God, this kind of distinction does not exist. With any of His divine senses, He can do the work of all of them.

5. *Avraṇam.* Without wounds, unscathed.

Some scholars explain the previous word, *akāyam*, to mean 'God does not have a body.' But then *avraṇam* would make no sense. When already stated 'He does not have a body,' then why say, 'His body is without wounds?' This is like the conversation:

'Has Ramesh come?'

'Yes, Ramesh has arrived.'

'Ok. So, have Ramesh's hands and feet also arrived?'

In this conversation, the second question is irrelevant. If Ramesh has arrived, his hands and feet have also arrived.

Likewise, if the previous attribute *akāyam* meant that God does not have a body, then this one—His body is *avraṇam* 'does not have wounds'—becomes irrelevant.

In reality, *akāyam* implies that God's body is not material; He has a spiritual body. Hence, *avraṇam* emphasizes the divinity of His body by saying that it is bereft of material defects.

6. *Asnāviram.* 'He is without veins and arteries.'

This again reinforces the idea that God's body is not material but spiritual. The Upanishad is expressing that His form is not made from the gross elements of the world. The *Padma Puran* details this point:

> *na tasya prākṛitī mūrtirmedomāmsāsthisambhavā*
>
> (5.77.43)

'The divine form of the Supreme Lord is free of flesh, blood, marrow, and organs that constitute material bodies.'

Thus, these three attributes of God's personal form refute the jnani's notion that God cannot possess a form.

***Kriya-vāchak nāma.* Names pertaining to God's divine activities.**

7. *Kaviḥ.* The word is composed from the roots *kavṛi* and *varṇane*. It means 'one who describes things as they are'. God manifested the Vedas from His breath, and this was the first time the Absolute Truth was revealed in our material universe. Thus, the Supreme Lord became the first *Kavi*.

From the perspective of grammar, 'ku' is the root, 'ach' is the suffix. The word *kavi* literally means 'one who knows'. The omniscient Lord is the original 'Knower and Revealer of the Truth'. He further imparted this knowledge to Shree Brahma. The Shreemad Bhagavatam states: *tene brahma hṛidāya ādikavaye* (1.1.1) 'At the beginning of creation, Narayan revealed the knowledge of the Vedas in the heart of the first-born, Shree Brahma. Thus, by Narayan's grace, Shree Brahma became the *ādi kavi*, "the first knower" in this Universe.'

Interestingly, *ādi kavi*, meaning 'first poet' has been a devotee of God in many of the Indian languages. For instance, Valmiki was the *ādi kavi* of Sanskrit literature. Narsi Mehta was the *ādi kavi* of Gujarati literature. The *ādi kavi* of Telugu literature was Nannaya. And Bhanubhakta Acharya, writer of the Nepali Ramayan, is considered the *ādi kavi* of Nepali.

The full import of *Kavi* in this mantra is that God Himself is the original Knower and Revealer of the Truth. From time to time, He creates *ādi kavis* in the world by His power, including *ādi kavi* Brahma.

8. *Manīṣhī.* 'The wise one who contemplates on deep principles.'

Who can be a bigger *manīṣhī* than God Himself? Whenever He descends on the earth as an Avatar, He shares deep philosophical truths, and humankind gains a veritable sea of knowledge. Through the philosophical discussion between Shree Ram and Guru Vasishth, we obtained a rare scripture, *Yog Vasishth.* When Shree Krishna became Arjun's guru and propounded philosophical truths to him, the world received the Bhagavad

Gita. Yet again, Maharshi Kapil, Who was also a descension of the Supreme, taught *Sankhya Darshan.*

Commentators have considered another meaning of the word *manīṣhī* in this mantra, as 'one who controls the mind'. Great sages who have mastered their mind are called *manīṣhī.* The Supreme Lord, however, is the Master of everyone's mind. In fact, the mind derives its power to think from God. The *Kenopanishad* states:

yanmanasā na manute yenāhurmano matam
tadeva brahma tvam viddhi nedam yadidamupāsate

(verse 1.5)

'The Supreme is beyond the mind's contemplation, for the mind itself derives its ability to think from Him. Hence, no one can challenge that they will know Him by the thinking power of their mind.'

Therefore, God is the primal and eternal *Manīṣhī* and the Source of everyone's ability to think.

9. *Paribhūḥ.* The word is composed from the root phrase *bhū sattāyām*. When used for God, it means 'He who is present everywhere at the same time.'

By His omnipresence, God maintains the world. This vast and complex creation could not have remained stable for even a moment, without His ubiquity in it. Just as a computer's circuitry is powered by electricity—and is useless and inert without it—likewise, the world too cannot function without God's all-pervading presence.

10. *Svayambhūḥ.* He who is his own cause.

Some interpret *svayambhū* to mean 'the sudden appearance of a powerful entity in the emptiness of space'. Further, they laughably opine that the said entity was subsequently worshipped as God.

However, the Vedas explain that 'space' is not mere nothingness. It also an entity, and it is manifest by God. In that space, creation of other entities proceeds. The *Taittiriya Upanishad* explains: 'From that Supreme, sky was created. From sky came the air; from the air came fire; from fire came water; from water came the earth; from earth came plants. And from plants, food was born.' (2.1.1)

Modern science has understood that space is not independent of time. Both are woven together in a space-time fabric. The Vedas inform that 'time' is also a creation of the Supreme. The *Atharvashira Upanishad* states:

akṣharāt sanjāyate kālaḥ (mantra 8)

'Time is born of the immortal Supreme Lord.' Thus, God is neither a product of the emptiness of space, nor is He a phenomenon occurring in time. On the contrary, God is the Creator of both space and time.

The idea behind calling God *svayambhū* is to indicate that He is self-manifest. Every entity in creation originates from Him, but He does not have a source. Thus, He is also referred to as 'The Cause of all causes'. This is how Shree Brahma prays to Him:

anādirādi govindaḥ sarvakāraṇa kāraṇam

(*Brahma Samhita* 5.1)

'Shree Krishna is the Origin of everything, but He Himself is without an origin. He is without a cause and is the Cause of all causes.'

The import is that no one manifested the Supreme—He is His own cause. In this manner, God is *Svayambhū*.

11. *Yathātathya arthān vyadadhātaḥ*. 'One who creates life materials, leading to the experience of joys and sorrows, for living entities based on their karmas.'

It is important to distinguish the usage of *arthān* here from other standard usages of the word. In Varnashrama dharma, there are four kinds of activities defined: *dharma*, *artha*, *kaam*, and *moksha*. The *arthān* appearing in this mantra does not refer to the *artha* that is a limb of the fourfold fruitive activities. Nor does it refer to *artha*, meaning 'economic resources'.

In this mantra, the word *arthān* encompasses all events, circumstances, destiny, ripened karmas, mental states, and destinations that are awarded to a living entity on the basis of its karmas.

However, the Law of Karma can only be administered by an all-knowing Entity Who keeps track of every thought and deed in every lifetime of every living entity. Also, it requires an all-powerful Entity to dispense the fruits of the karmas. Such an omniscient and all-powerful being is God alone. The mantra thus refers to Him as *yathātathya arthān vyadadhātaḥ*.

The above five activity-related names are proof that God possesses numerous shaktis for performing these tasks. This refutes the jnani's notion that God is *shakti rahit* i.e. 'without shakti'.

Moreover, to conduct activities at the scale of creation, an endless dynamism is necessary. This refutes the jnani's notion that the Supreme Lord is an inert inactive principle.

For the Scholars

It is important to note that no living entity in the material realm possesses the 11 attributes of God described in this mantra. But the question remains: what happens after salvation? Does the soul become Brahman?

Ved Vyas states in the *Brahma Sutra*: 'On realizing the Supreme, the soul relishes the infinite Bliss of God.' (4.4.21) *bhoga mātra sāmyalingāchcha.*

The God-realized soul receives divine love, divine knowledge, and divine bliss. This happens by the grace of God, through the Yogmaya shakti. However, the *Brahma Sutra* also states: 'The soul does not receive the powers of creation, maintenance, and dissolution of the world. These remain with the all-powerful God.' (4.4.17) *jagad-vyāpāra varjam.*

Hence, the distinction between jiva and Brahman persists even after God-realization. Thus, the unconditional equality of jiva and God is clearly refuted. Here are some more differences between God and the jiva:

- God is *svādhīn* (independent), while the jiva is *parādhīn* (dependent).
- God is the *niyāmak* (controller), while the jiva is *niyamy* (controlled) by Him.
- God is *vibhu-chit* (infinitely conscious), while the jiva is *aṇu-chit* (endowed with tiny consciousness).
- God is omnipresent, while the soul's consciousness pervades only in the body it inhabits.
- God is the *pālak* (guardian), while the soul is its *bālak* (child).
- God is *sarva śhaktimān* (possessor of infinite powers), while

the jiva is *alpa-śhaktimān* (possessing limited powers).

This mantra aimed at deepening our devotion to the Supreme by enhancing our understanding of His Divine Personality. The next mantra sheds light on the tussle between materialism and spirituality and teaches us not to create a dysfunctional imbalance on either side.

Mantra 9

अन्धं तमः प्रविशन्ति येऽविद्यामुपासते ।
ततो भूय इव ते तमो य उ विद्यायां रताः ॥ ९॥

andham tamaḥ praviśhanti ye 'vidyāmupāsate
tato bhūya iva te tamo ya u vidyāyām ratāḥ

andham—blind; *tamaḥ*—darkness; *praviśhanti*—attain; *ye*—those who; *avidyām*—material science; *upāsate*—worship; *tataḥ*—than that; *bhūyaḥ*—more; *iva*—like; *te*—they; *tamaḥ*—darkness; *ye*—those who; *u*—also; *vidyāyām*—spiritual science; *ratāḥ*—engaged.

They attain darkness, who worship and embrace material science alone. But those who concern themselves with spiritual science alone are plunged into even greater darkness.

This mantra recognizes the need for cultivating both the spiritual and material aspects of life. It cautions us against the disastrous results of ignoring either of these branches of knowledge.

Materialists believe that nothing exists in the world, except matter and its modifications. Chasing material progress, they dismiss notions of spirituality as imagination. They feel that the purpose of life is no more than acquiring possessions, relishing relationships, pursuing delights, and so on. While attempting to squeeze happiness from low-value activities, they feel no solid necessity for adhering to higher values.

On the flip side, adherents of spiritual traditions reject materialism as unnecessary. They assert that we are the soul, and we must not waste time on bodily pursuits. The body is prone to die one day, so it must not be pampered. Instead, we must accumulate spiritual treasures that will continue into the afterlife.

The tussle between materialism and spirituality is not new. Humanity has been embroiled in this debate for millennia. Charvak Muni, a famous Indian philosopher, propagated an extreme form of materialism. He set forth three main tenets, which are not different from today's scientific materialism. The first tenet lays the foundation of his school of thought:

yāvajjīvet sukham jīvet ṛiṇam kṛitvā ghṛitam pivet
bhasmībhūtasya dehasya punarāgamanam kutaḥ

(Charvak Siddhant)

'As long you live, enjoy your life. If drinking ghee gives you pleasure, drink it even if you have to take a loan to buy it. Upon death, when your body is cremated, it will turn to ashes. Where is the question of returning to the world again?'

The same ideology is expressed in modern times by the acronym YOLO, meaning 'You Only Live Once'. The idea conveyed is that we only have one life to live, so why worry about karmic consequences in the afterlife? Why not revel and make merry, since anyway we know of nothing beyond death?

Coming back to Charvak, his argument conveniently ignores the existence of a spiritual entity called the 'atma' or 'soul'. He assumes the body to be the self. Charvak's hypothesis, however, could be questioned thus: 'The ingredients that constitute the body do not possess life. Then what causes the presence of life in the body?'

Charvak responds with this logic:

jaḍabhūtavikāreṣhu chaitanyam yattu dṛiśhyate
tāmbūlapūgachūrṇānām yogād rāga ivotthitam kutaḥ

(Charvak Siddhant)

In this verse, he explains that betel leaf is green, while powdered betel nut is brown. But when they combine together in the form of *pān* (betel leaf) and consumed, it confers a reddish hue on the lips. Likewise, says Charvak, the ingredients of the body are devoid of consciousness but when brought together in the body, they produce life. Thus, consciousness is not the result of the soul or the presence of some non-material principle. The body is a bag of atoms and molecules, and that is all there is.

However, Charvak's hypothesis can again be questioned: 'Insentient substances are lifeless. Even when combined in the body, they cannot create life, as this is fundamentally different from their inherent nature.'

The Vedas declare the existence of the 'atma', which is immortal and eternal. They state that our present life is just one of the countless lives of our soul. We lived before our present birth, and 'death' will be nothing but the soul's departure from its present body.

On hearing such arguments, Charvak gets irate and presents his third tenet, very much along the lines of many materialists of today:

trayovedasya kartārau bhaṇḍadhūrtaniśhācharāḥ

(Charvak Siddhant)

'The composers of the three Vedas are cunning demons, endowed with a corrupted intellect.' Charvak claims the writers of the Vedas have created ideas, such as atma and Paramatma, heaven and hell, and virtue and sin to delude people. Interestingly, even today, materialists in India voice similar opinions about the Vedas.

In fact, the scientific materialism currently prevalent is also a polished version of Charvak's first two sutras. The underlying assumption in science is that all of creation is a result of material elements and their inherent energy. For example, modern physics concerns itself with only material substances. You never hear a scientist saying, 'This law came into existence by the power of God.'

While propounding its theories, science keeps no space for the existence of any transcendental principle. It conveniently assumes that over time, insentient materials have combined to yield complex life forms. Consciousness arose with the advent of the composite forms, and the continuous evolution of life forms has led to the appearance of human beings, endowed with finer sensibilities and intellect.

There is no denying the multitude of ways humankind has benefitted from scientific development. Thus, science must be accorded credit for enriching and transforming the quality of our life experience on earth. Yet, from the perspective of knowing the Absolute Truth, there are some leaps of faith made in science which are being questioned here. The big assumption is that non-conscious particles can combine to produce consciousness. This has never been proved; nobody has ever combined atoms and molecules to create life. Scientist Thomas Huxley expressed it well:

> If you were to ask a scientist whether they believe in religion or spirituality. Invariably they would say, they do not believe. And if you were to ask them, "Do you possess a free will?" They would say, "Yes. we do."
>
> Intuitively we all know we do possess a free will. Yet, in the laws of nature known today, there is no scope for free will. Yet all scientists do realize that we do possess the freedom to choose. This or that.

The vital point Huxley made was that science has no explanation for the existence of free will. Huxley did not, however, notice an even bigger lacuna in the epistemology of science—the inability to explain the origin of 'awareness' in living beings. While we make complex gadgets using sophisticated technology, can we make a gadget that is 'aware'?

Humankind has now developed artificial intelligence (AI). But is AI aware of what it does? Of course not. While it uses vector algorithms, etc., to arrive at answers, it does not possess the quality of 'life', which is 'consciousness'. Albert Szent-Györgyi, Nobel Prize winner in physiology, stated:

> ...in my search for the secret of life, I ended up with atoms and electrons, which have no life at all. Somewhere along the line life has run out through my fingers. So, in my old age, I am now retracing my steps, trying to fight my way back.[12]

Apart from the philosophical incompleteness, materialism suffers from another shortcoming. It cannot entirely solve the problem of mental distress and emotional misery. All around us, we see how even most apparently successful people are prey to stress, anxiety, envy, and resentment so much so that they cannot sleep at night without consuming sedatives.

Thus, it becomes clear that external progress alone will not suffice in remedying the problems of life. This explains the first line of the mantra: 'They attain darkness, who worship and embrace material science alone.'

Let us now understand the perspective of spiritualists. The word 'spirituality', or *adhyātmavāda*, can etymologically be split into *adhi* (completely), plus *atma* (soul), plus *vāda* (philosophy). It literally means 'philosophy that is entirely focused on the soul'. Spiritualists believe that the body is mortal while the soul is immortal. So, we must strive to uplift our soul and not pamper the body.

However, some spiritualists take this argument to an extreme. They claim that since the body will perish one day, sole importance should be given to matters of the atma. Thinking

---

[12] Shanta, B.N., 'Life and consciousness—The Vedāntic view', *Communicative & integrative biology*, Vol. 8, No. 5, e1085138, 2015, https://doi.org/10.108/19420889.2015.1085138. Last accessed on 31 December 2024.

thus, they reject worldly pursuits to the extent of denying the day-to-day bodily requirements, fearing that such activities will pollute their consciousness with worldliness.

On the one side, materialists prioritize the external side of life, while ignoring their inner growth. On the other side, spiritualists deny the external world as an illusion and focus exclusively on inner purification. This mantra rejects both these extremes as incorrect.

Then, there are some spiritualists who accumulate the knowledge of the scriptures, but do not care to put it to practice. Their learning, being devoid of realization, leads to pride. Furthermore, on the basis of their bookish knowledge, fanatical theologians engage in unnecessary debates, taking great delight in their victory over novice scholars and the unhappiness they cause.

Factually, spiritual learning is not just about putting ideas into our head, but about assimilating them into our heart and implementing them in our actions. Empty knowledge is berated in the *Panchatantra*:

yathā kharaḥ chandana bhāravāhī,
bhārasya vettā na tu chandanasya
aevam hi śhāstrāṇi bahūni adhītya,
artheṣhu mūḍhāḥ kharavad vahanti

'A donkey laden with a load of sandalwood is only aware of its weight and knows nothing about its soothing effect. Likewise, foolish people who read various scriptures, but do not put the knowledge to practice, are no better than donkeys.'

There are other spiritualists who prematurely abandon worldly duties, though they remain slaves to their minds and senses. Such hypocrites pretend to be elevated sadhaks and busy themselves in creating a flock of like-minded hypocrites. The *Ramcharitmanas* describes this phenomenon:

nāri muī gṛiha sampati nāsī
mūḍa muḍāi hohin saṅyāsī (*Uttara Kand* 7.99.3)

'A man's wife died or he went bankrupt, so he shaved his head and became a monk. In the age of Kali, such hypocrites—with matted hair and long fingernails—are acclaimed as austere sages, based on external renunciation.'

Berating such empty theologians and pretentious scholars, the mantra says: *tato bhūya iva te tamo ya u vidyāyam ratāḥ* 'The so-called spiritualists who misuse their *shastra jnana* to bring suffering upon themselves and others attain deeper darkness.' In this way, extremes on both sides of the spectrum are derided.

For the Scholars

Let us delve deeper into Charvak's philosophy. Etymologically, *chāruvāka* is a person who speaks *vāk* (words) that are *chāru* (liked by people). The Sanskrit dictionary explains:

chāruḥ lokasammato vāko vākyam yasya saḥ chāruvākaḥ

'One who speaks words that are liked by people and appeal to the masses, is described as *chāru-vāk*.' With the passage of time, *chāru-vāk* became *Chārvāka* or Charvak.

The Puranas relate a humorous story explaining the origin of Charvak's philosophy. Astonishingly, it was first taught by Deva Guru, Brihaspati, to the *asura* society. Why did the Deva Guru teach such a reductionist viewpoint? Let us see.

During the devāsura sangrām—*battle between celestials and demons—a stage came when many* asuras *perished, tilting the odds of victory in favour of the gods. At this point Shukracharya, the guru of the demons, decided to intervene. He departed into the forest to perform penance and gain* Sañjīvanī Vidyā, *with the help of which he would revive the fallen* asuras.

When Brihaspati came to know of Shukracharya's plan, he thought, 'With great difficulty the demons have been felled. If they get revived, it will result in a major calamity for the devatas.' So, he pre-empted the asura *guru. Deceitfully taking the form of Shukracharya, Brihaspati went in the midst of the remaining* asuras. *They thought their teacher had returned and welcomed him with reverence.*

Then Brihaspati, in the form of Shukracharya, announced, 'I am back from my penances and have learnt the way to the highest welfare. For a happy life, we must eat, drink, and enjoy. There is no such thing called atma. The Vedas and other scriptures are all false.' Saying this, Brihaspati got the bodies of slain asuras *cremated, and left, thus saving the devas from defeat.*

When Shukracharya returned and learnt what had happened, he tried his best to remove Brihaspati's teachings from the intellects of the asuras, *but by then it had become firmly established in their consciousness.*

***Avidya* also means 'Vedic rituals'.** Shankaracharya explains the mantra from this perspective. This interpretation is also valid, so let us try to understand it.

As per Shankaracharya, *vidya* is 'spiritual knowledge', while *avidya* is 'Vedic rituals'. He then describes the darkness that accrues from them. The result of karm-kand i.e. 'rituals prescribed in the Vedas' is not self-realization.

svarga kāmo yajeta (*Mimansa Darshan* 6.1.1)

'Perform yajnas with the desire to go to the celestial abodes.'

The fruit of ritualistic practices is the attainment of celestial abodes, for a limited time, until one's pious merits are depleted. From this perspective, the practice of karm-kand which is devoid of bhakti will not solve the problem of material bondage. Hence, the *Mundakopanishad* states:

avidyāyāmantare vartamānāḥ
svayam dhīrāḥ paṇḍitammanyamānāḥ
dandramyamāṇāḥ pariyanti mūḍhā
andhenaiva nīyamānā yathāndhāḥ (1.2.5)

'Those who make Vedic rituals their primary focus and consider themselves as learned—without engaging in spiritual practice—are akin to a blind man who shows the way to other blind men. Such people come back in the cycle of birth and death, time and again.'

The Bhagavad Gita also strongly dissuades us from getting entangled in rituals for fruitive rewards:

yāmimām puṣhpitām vācham pravadanty-avipaśhchitaḥ
veda-vāda-ratāḥ pārtha nānyad astīti vādinaḥ (2.42)

'Men of small knowledge are very much attached to the flowery words of the Vedas, which recommend various fruitive activities for elevation to heavenly planets, resultant good birth, power, and so forth.'

In conclusion, the fruitive rituals described in the Vedas do not liberate us from maya; we continue transmigrating in the cycle of life and death. Hence, Shankaracharya opines this is the darkness of material existence that the *Ishopanishad* is talking about.

Having cautioned the reader about the harmful effects of the two extremes—rampant materialism and unbalanced spirituality—the Upanishad now explains the need for the proper use of both spiritual and material knowledge.

Mantra 10

अन्यदेवाहुर्विद्ययाऽन्यदाहुरविद्यया ।
इति शुश्रुम धीराणां ये नस्तद्विचचक्षिरे ॥ १०॥

anyadevāhurvidyayā 'nyadāhuravidyayā
iti śhuśhruma dhīrāṇām ye nastadvichachakṣhire

anyat—other; *eva*—certainly; *āhuḥ*—said; *vidyayā*—by spiritual science; *anyat*—other; *āhuḥ*—said; *avidyayā*—by material science; *iti*—thus; *śhuśhruma*—heard; *dhīrāṇām*—from equipoised; *ye*—who; *naḥ*—to us; *tat*—that; *vichachakṣhire*—explained.

The practices of *vidya* (spiritual science) and *avidya* (material science) bestow very different fruits. The enlightened and equipoised saints have explained this in detail.

Our inner experience reveals that without spiritual wisdom, material progress does not bestow fulfillment. However, our everyday experience also reveals that given the complexity of our body, it is foolish to renounce material science. Both *vidya* and *avidya,* have their relevance and importance in our everyday life. This is the subject of discussion in the present mantra.

Spiritual practitioners require material knowledge for bodily maintenance. Mahakavi Kalidas states in *Kumarsambhava*: *śharīram ādyam khalu dharma sādhanam* 'The body is the vehicle for engaging in religious activity.' If it becomes unwell, spiritual pursuits too get impeded. A mere toothache can fill the heart with pain, making it difficult to remember God. The *Ramcharitmanas* states: *tana binu beda bhajana nahin baranā* (*Uttara Kand* 7.95.3) 'The Vedas do not recommend we ignore the body while engaging in spirituality.'

We must take care of our body, providing it with its required nourishment. A plant requires many things for its survival—if you surround it with water alone, it will die. Similarly, the body too requires proper nutrition, yoga, pranayam, sleep, and more. The Bhagavad Gita attests to this:

nātyaśhnatastu yogo 'sti na chaikāntam anaśhnataḥ
na chāti-svapna-śhīlasya jāgrato naiva chārjuna (6.16)

'O Arjun, those who eat too much or too little, sleep too much or too little, cannot attain success in Yog.' Thus, the bodily needs of food and exercise must be met.

In fact, the impact of food goes beyond the body and even affects the mind. The *Chhandogya Upanishad* teaches through this story.

Guru Uddalak explained the importance of diet to his disciple, Shwetaketu. He said: āhāra śhuddhau sattva śhuddhiḥ (7.26.2) *'If you eat pure food, your mind will get purified.'*

Shwetaketu questioned how the mind could be affected by one's diet. Gurudev instructed him to conduct an experiment by undertaking a fast. On the 15th day, Uddalak asked him to relate memorized Vedic mantras, but Shwetaketu had forgotten them. Gurudev then asked him to break his fast. When nourished, Shwetaketu was able to remember the mantras again. In this way, the importance of one's diet was proved. Because the same mantra further explains sattvaśhuddhau dhruvā smṛitiḥ *'With a nourished and purified mind, the memory becomes powerfully responsive'.*

The Vedas explain that the food we consume gets divided in three ways: the subtlest portion builds the mind; the less subtle portion builds the body; and the gross portion is expelled as waste. This link between diet and the mind is the reason why excessive consumption of chillies is correlated to greater propensity for anger. So, for example, understanding diet, cooking, purchasing, etc. requires worldly knowledge.

The takeaway is that *avidya*—material science—cannot be rejected. If spiritual practitioners decry it, they are mistaken. Ask those who assert that Brahman is the only reality and the world is an illusion, to stop eating for a week, and they will soon realize the importance of the world.

On the flip side, however, materialists who deny the need for spirituality are also mistaken. No matter how much we enrich our standard of living, it cannot bestow peace and contentment, simply because happiness is not a product of the luxuries we possess; it hinges upon the state of our own mind. This subtle machine within us is vital to our life experience.

This is where material knowledge falls short. It does not possess the technology for controlling and managing our mind. Albert Einstein, the greatest scientist of the last century, expressed it very accurately: 'It is easier to denature plutonium than it is to denature the evil spirit of man.'[13]

Spiritual science addresses this aspect of the human experience. It is that body of knowledge which gives us the tools to purify our mind and intellect. We learn to manage our thoughts, to make them lofty and sublime. This, in-turn, helps us lead a noble life. Max Planck, famous quantum physicist, recognized this need for spirituality. In his book, *Where is Science Going?*,[14] he stated:

> There can never be any real opposition between religion and science; for the one is the complement of the other. Every serious and reflective person realizes, I think, that the religious element in his nature must be recognized and cultivated if all the powers of the human soul are to act together in perfect balance and harmony. And indeed it was not by accident that the greatest thinkers of all ages were deeply religious souls.

Second, material science is devoid of values. It places huge power in our hands but does not teach us how to discriminate between its good or bad use. This is why there is so much apprehension about the misuse of genetic engineering, stem cell technology, AI, and more. The wisdom for their ethical and

---

[13] Einstein, Albert, 'The Real Problem is in the Hearts of Men', *The New York Times Magazine*, 23 June 1946, https://www.nytimes.com/1946/06/23/archives/the-real-problem-is-in-the-hearts-of-men-professor-einstein-says-a.html. Last accessed on 9 January 2025.

[14] Planck, Max, and James Murphy (trans), *Where Is Science Going?*, W.W. Norton & Company Inc, New York, 1932, p. 168.

moral use requires spirituality.

In summary, humans need both *vidya* and *avidya* in their lives. However, the right use of *avidya* and *vidya* is an extremely nuanced science. It must be understood under the guidance of a guru.

Iti śhuśhruma dhīrāṇām in the mantra emphasizes the need for a guru. It suggests we learn spiritual wisdom from the wise ones.

The word *dhīr* used here is very significant. Etymologically, *dhāraṇā-śhakti* is the 'ability to retain'. Hence, *dhīr* is a person who has developed *dhṛiti* i.e. 'ability to retain'. In the spiritual context, those who harbour divine knowledge and divine love in the receptacle of their heart are the *dhīraṇām*. These are the spiritual masters who can teach us.

Dhīr is used for a guru in the *Ramcharitmanas* as well.

rāma sindhu ghana sajjana dhīrā
chandana taru hari santa samīrā

(*Uttara Kand* 7.119.9)

This chaupai uses such beautiful analogies for saints. 'If Bhagavan Ram is an Ocean, then His *dhīr* saints are the clouds that carry the waters of divine love to us. If Shree Ram is a sandalwood tree, then His *dhīr* devotees are the breeze that bring us the fragrance of His divine grace.'

For the guru, Shree Krishna uses two similar words—*jñāninaḥ* (those having knowledge of the scriptures) and *tattva darśhinaḥ* (those who have seen the Truth)—in the Bhagavad Gita:

tad viddhi praṇipātena paripraśhnena sevayā
upadekṣhyanti te jñānaṁ jñāninas tattva-darśhinaḥ (4.34)

'Learn the Truth by approaching a spiritual master. Inquire from him with reverence and render service unto him. Such an enlightened saint can impart knowledge unto you because he has seen the Truth.'

The gurus who explain the science of God-realization are very benevolent. The *Gopi Geet* praises them, saying: 'Those who explain the divine pastimes of God are *bhūridā janāḥ* or "most benevolent".'

In the Indian culture, therefore, the spiritual master who helps us unite with God is accorded high respect. *Guruḥ sākṣhāt parabrahma tasmai śhrī gurave namaḥ* (*Guru Gita*, *Skanda Puran*) 'I bow down to the guru, who is a veritable form of the Supreme Brahman.'

The Upanishad thus encourages us to find a true guru—who is most benevolent—and learn from him how to practise spirituality in a balanced manner.

Having explained the need for both material and spiritual sciences in our everyday life, the next mantra will reveal the process of achieving this synthesis between these two branches of knowledge and the fruit of such balanced living.

Mantra 11

विद्यां चाविद्यां च यस्तद्वेदोभयं सह ।
अविद्यया मृत्युं तीर्त्वा विद्ययामृतमश्नुते ॥ ११॥

vidyām chāvidyām cha yastadvedobhayaṁ saha
avidyayā mṛityum tīrtvā vidyayāmṛitamaśhnute

vidyām—spiritual science; *cha*—and; *avidyām*—material science; *cha*—and; *yaḥ*—one who; *tat*—that; *veda*—knows; *ubhayam*—both; *saha*—in unison; *avidyayā*—by material science; *mṛityum*—death; *tīrtvā*—transcend; *vidyayā*—by spiritual science; *amṛitam*—deathlessness; *aśhnute*—enjoys.

Those who adopt both *vidya* and *avidya* in unison, such expert spiritual seekers, navigate the world with the help of material science and reach the eternal abode of God through spiritual science.

The *Ishopanishad* continues its reconciliation of opposites. In this mantra, the Upanishad explains the perfect synthesis of both spirituality and materialism. It teaches us how to utilize both *vidya* and *avidya* for our benefit.

- *Avidya* i.e. material knowledge enables us to understand external nature and harness it for the necessities of our body.
- *Vidya* or spiritual knowledge helps us comprehend our inner nature—the mind, intellect, and ego—and purify it to manifest the divinity of the soul within.

Thus, both are relevant and beneficial for successful living. The *Mundaka Upanishad* explains: *dve vidye veditavye...parā chaivāparā cha* 'Both material science and spiritual science are valid branches of human knowledge.' Just as a train runs on two tracks, we too must utilize both disciplines.

Let us examine the life of the Buddha. When he witnessed the defects of human existence—birth, disease, old age, and death—he renounced the world. Subsequently, he relinquished efforts to maintain the body. Engaging in intense austerities in the forests, he ignored all bodily needs to the point that He grew weak. With the onset of hunger and dizziness, meditation expectedly became a formidable challenge.

One day, some village women were singing a song as they passed by. The meaning was: 'Tighten the strings of the tanpura (Indian musical instrument) and make them sound sweet. But do not tighten them so much that they break.'

On hearing this, the Buddha had a profound realization. He thought, 'This wisdom applies to the body too. We must tighten it through austerities, but not to the extent that the body itself perishes.'

In His subsequent efforts, the Buddha was mindful of his physical needs for maintenance. He made it one of the core insights in his ideology, which became known as the '**Middle Path**'.

Interestingly, the ancient Greek philosopher, Aristotle, used almost similar terminology. Advocating the principle of the '**golden mean**', he spoke against both gross avidity and extreme denial.

In balancing the material and the spiritual, a caution is worth mentioning. Accept materialism only to the extent that it meets your basic bodily and comfort needs. Else, desires will never cease, and you will end up chasing the ever-receding mirage of future happiness. Therefore, be wise and keep material pursuits within reasonable limits.

On the other hand, keep progressing spiritually without limit. We can continue increasing it ad infinitum. Through spirituality we develop equanimity of mind, which improves our inner life and makes our thoughts exalted. The more we develop it, the greater control we will get over anger, greed, desire, and pride. As a result, we become more effective in our worldly duties as well.

Let us now take a deeper dive into the fruits of cultivating spiritual wisdom.

Spirituality helps develop good values and beliefs. As we go through life, we are presented with numerous options and are required to make choices.

– In this ethical dilemma, what is my duty?

– In the present situation, what should I prioritize and why?

– What should I make as the goal of my life?

If we do not have a system of beliefs to reference, making these choices can become overwhelming and impossible. Sacred books of spirituality, such as the Upanishads, offer us divine wisdom for our personal structure of beliefs. They reveal the values that great saints successfully practised. In this way, they clarify our path for moving ahead in life.

Spirituality helps us see the bigger picture. The demands of our daily routines entangle us in mundane tasks. We are obliged to run from morning till night to earn money. We are required to take care of our family. But while fulfilling these worldly necessities, we also have a need for a higher fulfillment, beyond the mundane. Spiritual wisdom helps us connect with elevated ideas and noble concepts.

Spirituality helps us become a better person. Deep within, we all aspire to become a better version of ourselves. Yet, self-transformation does not come easy. We struggle with negative thoughts and detrimental habits. In this situation, a good spiritual belief system hands us the tools and practices required for improving ourselves. It also strengthens our commitment to practising self-discipline in life. Consequently, our journey of inner purification speeds up.

It is a pity that despite all these benefits, spirituality is looked down upon in academic circles. To talk about the soul and God in corporate boardroom discussions or scientific interactions is considered old-fashioned. In India, in the name of secularism, spirituality has been eliminated from education. Students go through their entire school and college life without learning about spirituality.

Spirituality helps us attain the supreme goal of life. Without learning and practising it, we will keep rotating in the cycle of life and death in this material realm. As Shankaracharya said:

punarapi jananam punarapi maraṇam
punarapi jananī jaṭhare śhayanam (*Bhaja Govindam*)

'We are born, then one day we die, and then, hang upside down in a mother's womb.' This cycle has repeated itself innumerable times in the past and will continue until we attain the supreme realization.

Ultimately, the purpose of our human life is God-realization. Only then can we get the true bliss that our soul has been thirsting for since eternity. From this perspective, spirituality is like the 'one', while everything else is like 'zeros'. With 'one' in the lead, every 'zero' behind it adds value. Without it, life remains zero—futile and purposeless.

Amṛitmaśhnuteḥ. This word informs us that *vidya* will bestow eternal life. When we learn spiritual science and put it to practice, our mind will get purified. This then attracts divine grace and leads to God-realization. Thus, the *Rig Veda* states:

ṛite jñānānna muktiḥ

'Without spiritual knowledge, it is impossible to get liberated from the bondage of maya.' The Bhagavad Gita states:

na hi jñānena sadṛiśham pavitramiha vidyate (4.38)

'In the entire world, there is nothing as beneficial and purifying as spiritual knowledge.'

Through this mantra, we have learnt the syncretic approach between material and spiritual sciences. We have also learnt the need for balancing both *avidyā* and *vidya* in our life, to achieve health, happiness, and spiritual fulfillment.

For the Scholars

Why does the *Ishopanishad* refer to spiritual science alone as *vidya*? Can other branches of knowledge also be called by the same name, e.g. the *vidya* of music or the *vidya* of dance?

The answer to this question requires comprehending the Vedic definition of *vidya*. The root *vit* means 'knowledge imbued with experience'. *Samvit* means *jāgrati* or 'knowledge that leads to awakening'. Thus, knowledge which awakens the soul from its ignorance and leads to appreciation of divine principles, can be termed as *vidya*.

The *Vishnu Puran* provides a beautiful explanation:

tatkarma yanna bandhāya sā vidyā yā vimuktaye (1.19.41)

'That alone is *karm* which does not entangle us in bondage. That alone is *vidya* which frees us from the bondage of maya.'

Vidya is, hence, the spiritual science that will result in *mṛityum tīrtvā*, i.e. 'freedom from death'.

Having examined the topic of vidya *and* avidya, *the Upanishad next does the same analysis for* sambhūti *and* asambhūti. *In the process, we get to know where we should focus our devotion and where we should not.*

Mantra 12

अन्धं तमः प्रविशन्ति येऽसम्भूतिमुपासते ।
ततो भूय इव ते तमो य उ सम्भूत्यां रताः ॥ १२॥

andham tamaḥ praviśhanti ye 'sambhūtimupāsate
tato bhūya iva te tamo ya u sambhūtyāṁ ratāḥ

andham—ignorance; *tamaḥ*—darkness; *praviśhanti*—attain; *ye*—those who; *asambhūtim*—originated beings; *upāsate*—worship; *tataḥ*—than that; *bhūyaḥ*—more; *iva*—like; *te*—those; *tamaḥ*—darkness; *ye*—who; *u*—also; *sambhūtyām*—in the Absolute; *ratāḥ*—engaged.

Those who worship originated beings attain darkness. However, those who worship the eternal Lord—with pride and arrogance—end up in far greater darkness.

The concepts of *vidya* and *avidya* were discussed in the previous triad of mantras, from 9 to 11. With this 12th mantra begins a second triad that delves into the concepts of *sambhūti* and *asambhūti*.

Let us start the discussion by understanding the terms that have been employed herein.

Upasana comes from the root *āsana*, which implies 'to sit'. The prefix *upa* means 'near'. Hence, *upasana* means 'to go and sit close'. From a spiritual perspective, *upasana* implies 'to take your mind to something'.

We souls can either take our mind to God or to His created world. The mantra refers to these two realms by the terms—*sambhūti* and *asambhūti*. First, we will understand their meaning, and then the idea of the mantra will be clear.

Sambhūti implies *svatantra sambhava*, meaning 'of independent origin'. God alone is *sambhūti* since He is the Cause of all causes. He does not owe His origin to any other entity.

Asambhūti means 'not of independent origin'. All living beings and objects in this material world are *asambhūti*. They have come into existence from God, Who is the original Source of everything.

Worship of *asambhūti* (*asambhūti upasana*) means 'to attach the mind to objects or living beings of the world'. Included in this are celestial gods, ancestors, humans, ghosts, and material objects.

The mantra starts by saying *asambhūti upasana* will result in darkness. Why is this so? As per the scriptures, our destination in the afterlife is decided by the object to which our mind is attached at the time of death.

The Puranas relate the story of Bharat Maharaj. Though he was a powerful king, he renounced his kingdom and went into the forest to practise sadhana. All was going well, until one day, he saw a newly born baby deer floating in the river. Moved by pity, he rescued the fawn and brought it to his hut. He began tending to it with great affection, but in the process, his mind came away from spiritual contemplation and got absorbed in the deer.

In his final moments, when Bharat was dying, the only thoughts in his mind were, 'How is the deer? What will happen to it after I leave?' Consequently, in his next life, Bharat was born as a deer.

The story illustrates the principle enunciated in the Bhagavad Gita:

yam yam vāpi smaran bhāvam tyajatyante kalevaram
tam tam evaiti kaunteya sadā tad-bhāva-bhāvitaḥ (8.6)

'Whatever one remembers upon giving up the body at the time of death, one attains that state, always absorbed in such contemplation.'

Let us understand the principle through the analogy of a father living in a small village, with four daughters. He marries his first daughter to a brilliant lad who clears the Indian Administrative Services (IAS) exam and becomes a government officer. People call the officer as sahib *i.e. 'sir', and his wife is addressed as* memsahib *i.e. 'madam'.*

The second daughter gets married to an office clerk. People call him 'babu', *while his wife gets the epithet* 'babuain' (terminology used in Uttar Pradesh).

The third is wedded to a drunkard, who later becomes impoverished. He is now known as bhikhari *i.e. 'beggar', while people speak of his wife as* bhikharin *i.e. 'beggar lady'.*

The fourth daughter gets wedded to a saint. He became the guru of a large congregation, and his wife is known as 'guru ma'.

Observe the huge difference in designations amongst the four daughters, though they all had the same father.

Like the daughters in the above example, is our mind, and like their husbands, are the personalities to whom we attach our mind. This can also be compared to a train with an engine and carriages. Wherever the engine goes, the carriages follow. The Bhagavad Gita again explains:

yānti deva-vratā devān pitṝīn yānti pitṛi-vratāḥ
bhūtāni yānti bhūtejyā yānti mad-yājino 'pi mām (9.25)

'Worshippers of the devatas take birth amongst them, worshippers of the ancestors go to their abode, worshippers of ghosts take birth amongst disembodied beings, and My devotees come to Me alone.'

Let us now individually look at the different kinds of *asambhūti upasana*.

Worship of the celestials. These are the devatas, such as Indra, Varun, Kuber, Agni, Vayu, and so on. They live in the higher planes of existence within this material world, called *swarg*. The devatas are not God; they are souls like us. They occupy specific posts in the administration of the world.

Some worship the celestial gods for material rewards. We must remember that these devatas cannot grant either liberation from material bondage or God-realization. Hence, the ultimate goal of the soul is not achieved. At best, the worshipper of the devatas may go to the celestial abodes after death. This is only for a finite amount of time, and then one has to return to the earth. *Svargau svalpa anta dukhadāī* (*Ramcharitmanas Uttara Kand* 7.43.1) 'Even the attainment of the joys of heaven is for a brief while, and then misery awaits.'

Worship of Ancestors. Those who live as per Varnashrama dharma, discharging their duties with diligence and faith, but are unable to conquer their attachments, go to *Pitṛi Lok*, the abode of the ancestors, on the strength of their karmas. Their attachment continues towards past family and clan, whom they had served dutifully in the previous life.

Some appease their family ancestors to benefit from their energies and gain desired results. These ancestors are less powerful than the celestial gods. When propitiated by karm-kand, they deploy their energies to bestow material rewards. However, taking aid of such ancestors results in both sides further strengthening their attachment based on material identity, which becomes a roadblock in spiritual upliftment.

Worship of humans. Living in the world, we become attached to family members, relatives, friends, and others. The attachment that we harbour towards them—for the sake of our pleasure—is the worship of humans. In our infatuation, we forget that all worldly relationships are temporary, and everyone will leave one day. Shankaracharya puts them in perspective in his poem *Bhaja Govindam*:

kā te kāntā kaste putraḥ
sansāro 'yamatīva vichitraḥ
kasya tvam vā kuta āyātaḥ
tatvam chintaya tadiha bhrātaḥ (verse 8)

'Who is your spouse? Who is your child? Strange are the ways of the world. O soul! think who you are, and where you have come from. O brother! Contemplate over these truths.'

We can compare relationships on earth to bonds forged in a train journey. When a fellow passenger's station arrives, they have to deboard, and we must now continue on our own. Similarly, we form ephemeral relationships in every life that end with death.

Worship of ghosts and spirits. Some persons, who are in tamasic consciousness, misuse tantra to invoke disembodied beings and extract favours from them. They either gain control over spirits themselves or take refuge of a spirit worshipper.

They do not realize that the worship of ghosts and spirits has disastrous consequences. As per the Law of Karma, such worshippers become indebted to spirits and reincarnate as one of them. Further, those who frequent such spirit worshippers also end up in a hellish birth.

These are the major categories of *asambhūti*. We have seen how worship of *asambhūti* keeps us in the samsara of repeated birth and death. From this perspective, the first line of the mantra says: *andham tamaḥ praviśhanti* 'It results in darkness.'

Now, let us come to the second line of this mantra.

Worship of Sambhūti (*sambhūti upasana*) means 'to take your mind to God'. This is devotion to God—His names, forms, virtues, pastimes, abodes, and saints. It purifies our mind and unites the soul with the Supreme.

If our mind is attached to God at death—His names, forms, virtues, pastimes, abodes, and saints—we shall attain Him. Hence, the fruit of *sambhūti upasana* i.e. worship of the Supreme, is God-realization. In conclusion, to achieve the supreme goal, we should worship *sambhūti* alone and no one else.

A question may be asked at this point: 'If we do not worship the devatas and ancestors, will they become upset, and will it be considered a sin?' The scriptures tell us not to worry. Worship of God takes care of everything. Consider the analogy of a tree, with its roots, leaves, fruit, and flowers. You do not have to water every leaf; simply irrigate the root of the tree, and the water will naturally reach all its parts. Likewise, the *Skanda Puran* states:

> *archite devadeveśhe śhankha chakra gadādhare*
> *architāḥ sarva devāḥ syuryataḥ sarvagato hariḥ*

'Simply worship Narayan, Lord of the devas, Who is adorned with the conch, disc, and mace, and is all-pervading. In His worship, the devas will automatically be worshipped.'

The conclusion is that we must only worship *sambhūti*. But look at the surprise! This mantra declares: *tato bhūya iva te tamo ya u sambhūtyāṁ ratāḥ* 'They enter into an even greater darkness' who worship *sambhūti*. What could be the reason for this contradiction? Let us find out.

When materially conditioned souls begin engaging in bhakti, the flaws of egotism, hypocrisy, jealousy, and the like, do not immediately go away. Devotion is not a sudden leap from sinner to saint; it is a journey that gradually takes us from impiety to holiness. Thus, the initial stage of bhakti is called *anarth nivṛitti* i.e. the phase when the defects are gradually falling away. In this stage of the journey, the devotee must be very careful to keep weeding out impurities from their heart. For example, when one plants paddy, wild grass also begins to grow with it. Ironically, these weeds grow even faster than the grain. Thus, a diligent farmer carefully plucks out the wild plants, which would otherwise outgrow the rice, choking it out.

Unfortunately, some sadhaks are negligent about the impurities within. They do not exercise care to weed out insincerity, pride, and hypocrisy from their heart. Contaminations then begin to dominate their consciousness until ulterior motives override the original intention of devotion.

Derailed from real bhakti, such aspirants start using devotion as a way to impress others and garner praise for themselves. Desiring to hear their own glories, they make a show of their bhakti, with hypocrisy and ostentation. While appearing to be *siddhas* externally, their heart remains filled with worldliness. The objective of pleasing God and guru no longer remains, instead they aim to please themselves.

Warning us of self-styled devotees in Kali yug, the *Ramcharitmanas* states:

jāken nakha aru jaṭā bisālā,
soi tāpasa prasiddha kalikālā (*Uttara Kand* 7.97.4)

'In the age of Kali, hypocrites with matted hair and long fingernails will be regarded as holy men of repute.' This kind of utilization of *sambhūti* for self-gratification is even more dangerous than the selfish use of *asambhūti.*

Thus, while the first line of this mantra warns us about attaching the mind to the world, the second line cautions us about engaging in false devotion to God.

This mantra explained the dangers in the worship of the world and also in the incorrect worship of God. The Upanishad now explains the end result of worshipping the world, and how it is different from the end result of worshipping God.

Mantra 13

अन्यदेवाहुः सम्भवादन्यदाहुरसम्भवात् ।
इति शुश्रुम धीराणां ये नस्तद्विचचक्षिरे ॥ १३॥

anyadevāhuḥ sambhavādanyadāhurasambhavāt
iti śhuśhruma dhīrāṇām ye nastadvichachakṣhire

anyat—other; *eva*—certainly; *āhuḥ*—said; *sambhavāt*—by worshipping the creator; *anyat*—other; *āhuḥ*—said; *asambhavāt*—by worshipping what is not God; *iti*—thus; *śhuśhruma*—by listening; *dhīrāṇām*—from the true gurus; *ye*—who; *naḥ*—unto us; *tat*—about that; *vichachakṣhire*—explained.

One result is obtained by worshipping the Supreme, Who is the Origin of all. A very different outcome accrues by

worshipping created beings. This we have understood by listening to the true gurus.

The previous mantra warned against attaching the mind to the world. Does this mean we should fear the world and run away from it? Quite the contrary. Since God pervades every atom of creation, the world itself is not inauspicious, nor can it be the reason for our sorrows.

The error we make is in harbouring the wrong attitude towards the world. Instead of utilizing it for a higher purpose, we try to enjoy it for fleeting delights. The Sanskrit words *upayog* (to utilize) and *upabhog* (to enjoy) explain this difference perfectly. Consider the following example.

A village in rural India had no wells, so the villagers would fetch water from the river a kilometre away. They approached a philanthropist with their problem, who constructed a well near their homes.

All was fine for a while until one of the villagers fell into the well and drowned. The other villagers accused the philanthropist, 'It is all your fault! If you had not built the well, the poor fellow would not have died.'

'The fault is not mine, but yours,' responded the benevolent man. 'I built the well as a favour for you to utilize. If one of you was careless and fell down, it is not my fault but yours.'

Like the village well is the world God has made for the evolution of the souls. Instead of its *upayog* for a higher purpose, we are trying to do its *upabhog* for sensual enjoyment. And when it results in misery, we blame external things. However, in this very world, the great saints also lived, and they were perfectly blissful. In fact, they saw the presence of the Divine in all things.

This means that the reason for our unhappiness is not the external world but the inner world within our mind. It is filled with desire, anger, and greed. This is why the *Maitreyi Upanishad* states: *chittmeva hi sansāraḥ tatprayatnena śhodhayet* 'The bondage you experience is because of the world within you. This inner world is the one you must strive to purify.'

We create the inner world with our mind which produces our perceptions of happiness and distress. This mind is so important that both bondage and liberation are dependent on our mind. The *Panchadashi* says:

mana eva manuṣhyāṇām kāraṇam bandha mokṣhayoḥ

'The mind is the cause of bondage, and the mind is the cause of liberation.' As gardeners of the mind, we must carefully tend to it and make it bloom with sublime thoughts and noble emotions.

How to purify the mind. It is in the factory of the mind that our thoughts are produced. Motivational speakers worldwide urge people to improve the quality of their thoughts. These messages are nice to listen to, but the problem arises in their implementation. Unless the mind gets purified, it cannot generate noble thoughts. So, how can we clean our mind? On this point, personality development coaches do not have an answer.

Actually, the simple straightforward solution is what the mantra teaches—*sambhūti upasana* i.e. 'devotion to God'. The Lord is all-pure, and when we attach our mind to Him, the mind too becomes purified. The process is explained in the Bhagavad Gita:

mām cha yo 'vyabhichāreṇa bhakti-yogena sevate
sa guṇān samatītyaitān brahma-bhūyāya kalpate (14.26)

'Those who serve Me with unalloyed devotion rise above the three modes of material nature and come to the level of the Brahman.' Presently, our mind is under the influence of the three modes of maya—sattva, rajas, and tamas—while God is transcendental to them. By devoting ourselves to the Lord, our mind will also be raised to the transcendental platform.

In this way, *sambhūti upasana* purifies our mind and takes us closer to Him. Ultimately one day, the mind becomes fully surrendered to God, and the state of *māmekam śharaṇam vraja* is reached. This is the state of complete *sharanagati*, at which point the divine grace of the Lord intervenes and one achieves God-realization. This is the divine outcome the mantra refers to.

Ananya bhakti. Is devotion to God something we are learning about for the first time? Most likely not. If you have the spiritual thirst to read the *Ishopanishad*, it is highly likely that you have strong spiritual sanskars. It is also likely that you have engaged in devotion in past lives as well, and this has resulted in your present quest for God.

So, we did engage in *sambhūti upasana* in many lifetimes, and yet we did not obtain the divine result. This was because of one mistake. In our devotion to the Lord, we were not *ananya*. What does this mean? We attached our mind partially to God, but also allowed it to cling to the world. And the scriptures say that this kind of equivocal devotion will not do. The *Ramcharitmanas* states:

chhūṭai mala ki malahi ke dhoeñ,
ghṛita ki pāva koi bāri biloeñ (*Uttara Kand* 7.48.3)

The verse explains that if you wash a cloth and also keep throwing ghee on it, the cloth will never become clean. Likewise, if you do bhakti of the Lord and also keep worldly attachments, the mind will not be purified. The world—including its personalities and things—is under the realm of the three gunas. Attaching the mind to it will keep our mind in the three gunas. In this scenario, devotion to the Lord will purify the mind, while love for the world will make it unclean again.

This is why the scriptures emphasize the condition of *ananyata.* The word comes from the roots *na,* meaning 'no' and *anya,* meaning 'other'. So *ananya bhakti* means that our love must be exclusively for God. The Shreemad Bhagavatam states: 'You must surrender to the Supreme alone, and then by His grace, you will go beyond fear and duality.' (11.12.15)

The *Taittiriya Upanishad* emphasizes this point in no uncertain words:

yadā hyevaiṣha aetasminnudaramantaram kurute. atha tasya bhayam bhavati (2.7.1)

'If there is even a hair's breadth of gap in the mind's attachment to God, fear of rebirth will remain.'

Hence, the *Ishavasya Upanishad* urges us to understand that love for the world will bestow a very different outcome than love for God. It will keep our mind impure and prevent us from achieving the supreme realization.

The second line of the mantra again brings in the concept of the guru.

Iti śhuśhruma dhīrāṇāṁ. In mantra 10, the word *dhīr* was explained as referring to a realized guru. Here, in mantra 13, the *Guru Tattva* is once again emphasized. The *Ishopanishad* is again encouraging us to learn the deep secrets of spirituality from a guru.

Many Upanishads have reiterated this principle in various places. For example, the *Chhandogya Upanishad* states: *āchāryavān puruṣho hi veda* (6.14.2) 'Only through a guru can you understand the Vedas.' So, let us go deeper into the *Guru Tattva.*

Why we need a guru. By itself, our intellect is incapable of knowing the Absolute Truth. As long as we are under maya, our intellect is afflicted by five defects. These are:

1) *Raga:* It is the attachment of our mind to objects and persons which has distorted our understanding. 2) *Dwesh:* This is the harbouring of bitterness and resentment. The intellect again gets distorted by it. 3) *Asmita:* This refers to the ego. It is our false sense of self-identity arising from identification with our possessions, designations, and so on. 4) *Abhinivesh:* The idea of death makes us paranoid, since we do not realize our soul is eternal. The apprehension of ceasing to exist forever naturally affects our values and perceptions. 5) *Avidya:* This is the nescience due to which we have forgotten our divine nature as 'atma'. Instead, we look upon ourselves as the body made of matter.

These five afflictions warp our intellect under maya, which is why, all the Vedic scriptures declare in unison that divine knowledge must be received from a guru.

anādy-avidyā-yuktasya puruṣhasyātma-vedanam
svato na sambhavād anyas tattva-jño jñāna-do bhavet
(verse 11.22.10)

The Shreemad Bhagavatam explains that we cannot acquire transcendental knowledge merely by our intellect, which is covered by nescience since endless lifetimes. Thus, we need a guru, who knows the Absolute Truth.

The same methodology for knowledge is enunciated in the *Panchadashi*:

tatpādāmburu hadvandva sevā nirmala chetasām
sukhabodhāya tattvasya viveko 'yam vidhīyate (1.2)

'Serve the guru with a pure mind, giving up doubts. He will then bring you great happiness by bestowing scriptural knowledge and discrimination.'

An interesting confirmation of the need for a guru comes from the divine leelas of Bhagavan Ram. During His descension on earth, He went to Guru Vasishth for knowledge. As God, He was omniscient; He did not need a guru's support for acquiring knowledge, yet He wished to establish a precedent for us to emulate. To teach us that we need the guidance of a guru, Lord Ram Himself received instruction at the feet of a guru.

Likewise, Shree Krishna also accepted a guru. He went to Sandipani Muni's *gurukul* in Ujjain, and there, He learnt 64 sciences in 64 days. How did He complete His education so quickly? The reason was that He did not actually require any study; He was merely enacting a pastime that would set an example for humanity.

Leaving no doubt regarding the necessity for a guru,

Shankaracharya states:

yāvat gururna kartavyo tāvanmuktirna labhyate
tasmāt guruśhcha kartavyo gurum̐ binā na siddhyati

'Unless one takes shelter of a guru, one cannot attain salvation. Hence, surrender to a guru, without whom you cannot achieve perfection.' Similarly, Saint Kabir says:

rāma rahe bana bhītare guru kī pūjā nā āsa
rahe kabīra pākhaṇḍa saba, jhūṭhe sadā nirāśha

'For those who say they do not need a guru because God is in the forest and elsewhere, Saint Kabir says that such people are hypocrites, and they are always disappointed.'

When we exert the intellect to grasp the guru's spiritual knowledge, we break free of our notions of sensual enjoyment and are instead adorned with the attitude of making the right and judicious use of *asambhūti*.

This mantra explained that worshipping God and worshipping the world bestow vastly different end results. The next mantra explains that we must reject neither of these realms; instead, learn to cultivate the proper mindset towards each. Then both these spheres add specific value to our life and help us attain the supreme destination.

Mantra 14

सम्भूतिं च विनाशं च यस्तद्वेदोभयं सह ।
विनाशेन मृत्युं तीर्त्वा सम्भूत्याऽमृतमश्नुते ॥ १४॥

sambhūtim cha vināśham cha yastadvedobhayaṁ saha
vināśhena mṛityum tīrtvā sambhūtyā 'mṛitamaśhnute

sambhūtim—the eternal God; *cha*—and; *vināśham*—the temporary world; *cha*—also; *yaḥ*—one who; *tat*—that; *veda*—to know and learn; *ubhayam*—both; *saha*—simultaneously; *vināśhena*—perishable; *mṛityum*—death; *tīrtvā*—crossover; *sambhūtyā*—from devotion to God; *amṛitam*—immortal; *aśhnute*—enjoy.

Learn to simultaneously engage in devotion to the eternal God, while judiciously using the temporary world. The proper use of the world will help you cross over the material realm of death, while devotion to the Supreme will bestow the bliss of the eternal realm.

This mantra uses the word *vināśham,* meaning 'destructible' for the world, while the previous two mantras had used the word *asambhūti* for the same. *Vināśham* is indeed a fitting appellation for worldly things. They have come into existence, and they will perish one day. Birth and death go hand in hand. The Bhagavad Gita sums it up very well:

nāsato vidyate bhāvo nābhāvo vidyate sataḥ (2.16)

'That which always existed, will never cease to be. But that which got created at a point of time, will surely perish one day.'

Creation and destruction come in pairs. Like we call the world 'creation', we can just as well call it 'destruction'. In conclusion, *asambhūti* and *vināśham* refer to the same material realm. This mantra has chosen to employ the word *vināśham* to emphasize temporariness. Previously, the use of '*asambhūti*' emphasized things have come into being, but it did not convey that they will perish. Only a rare scholar realizes the destructible side of *asambhūti*. Thus, for the desired impact, the mantra says *vināśham*.

The message is that all relationships and possessions in the world are temporary. Seeing them as destructible, we should not get attached, as was explained in the previous mantra too. Consider the following example.

Let us say, you go for a weekend vacation to a tourist place. You stay in a hotel room. Now, you do not bother if the curtains are not to your liking. Instead, you think, 'It is only a matter of two days, and then I will be on my way. Let me tolerate the room for what it is and focus on enjoying my vacation.'

Similarly, saints remind us that the world is a temporary abode. Jagadguru Kripaluji Maharaj states in His composition, *Radha Govind Geet*:

jaga men raho aise govinda rādhey,
dharmaśhālā men yātrī rahe jyaun batā de

'Live in the world as a traveller would live in a hotel.' Rather than accumulating treasures here—which we will leave behind at death—we should prioritize divine treasures that we will take along with us. Thinking in this manner, we should learn the proper use of things with a detached mind.

At this point, a question is asked: 'If we are not attached to our family and relatives, how will we do our duty towards them?' Well, the fact is that duty can be perfectly done when we are unattached. It is the clinging of our mind that creates all the stress and distress within us. Let me explain from a personal story.

Once, a middle-aged lady came to me, and said, 'I have too much anxiety.'

I asked her, 'What is your anxiety about, your children?'

'Yes,' she responded. 'How did you know?'

I explained that having been a spiritual counsellor for four decades, I was aware of the most common reason for anxiety in people of her age-group. Then I asked her what her profession was. She replied, 'I am a teacher. This year I was recognized for excellence in teaching and conferred an award.'

I then explained to her, 'You take care of a whole class of students with excellence and competence, but it does not give you anxiety. While at home, you have only 2–3 children, but taking care of them makes you anxious! This reveals the reason for your anxiety is attachment to your children. Now learn to simply do your duty towards them, with detachment, as you do for your students. This will prevent atrophy of the mind when it clings to material personalities.'

This is the wisdom we can infer from the mantra—neither run away from family and friends, nor be infatuated with them. Learn to handle relationships with detachment, and they will become much smoother. We will become happier and more effective in the world.

Consider another example of a nurse in a hospital. She does her duty towards the patients. She is diligent and sincere, but even while taking care of them, her mind is detached. If a patient dies, she does not lament; if a child is born, she does not rejoice. She simply performs her duty.

The Upanishad encourages us to work in the same manner, by making judicious use of the world. The works of the world will go on, but we will not be overwhelmed by anxiety, fear, apprehension, and stress. This will assist us in getting detached from the world, and we will cross over the material realm (*mṛityum tīrtvā*).

However, detachment alone does not suffice in attaining the supreme goal. It merely means that our running in the wrong direction has stopped. Consider the following example.

Suppose you begin driving south from Indore in Central India. A passerby asks you at a crossing, 'Sir, where are you headed to?'

'To Delhi,' you respond.

'In that case, you are headed in the wrong direction,' he informs. 'Delhi is to the north, and this road is going to Chennai in the south.'

On hearing the passerby, you stop your car. But merely stopping does not mean you have arrived in Delhi. It simply means your movement in the wrong direction has ceased. Now you need to find the right road to Delhi, and then proceed on it. Only then will you arrive at your destination.

Likewise, we want the bliss of the soul and are looking for it in the world. The Upanishad instructs us that loving the world will not bestow this fruit so, we become detached. But that is not enough. We must now find out how to attach the mind to God, and implement the instruction. Then we will attain the divine bliss we seek.

Hence, the mantra states that to reach our supreme destination, we must do *sambhūti upasana*. The *Ramcharitmanas* explains the same:

hima te anala prakaṭa baru hoī
bimukha rāma sukha pāva na koī

(*Uttara Kand* 7.121.10)

'Just as fire cannot manifest from ice, likewise, until we lovingly surrender to Bhagavan Ram, we cannot attain eternal bliss.' This present mantra of the *Ishopanishad* concludes with the same instruction: *sambhūtyā 'mṛitamaśhnute* 'Devotion to the Supreme will bestow the bliss of the eternal realm.'

In this way, mantra 14 gives us two tasks:

1) Make judicious use of the world, and

2) Love God with your mind.

Both these tasks must be done concurrently. This means that while working in the world, we must also keep our mind in God. Is this possible? Yes, it can be achieved by practising the principle of karm yog.

The technique of karm yog. To understand what this technique is, we must first appreciate *yog*. Nowadays, yoga has become a buzzword in the west. Yoga studios have mushroomed everywhere around the world. It is very heartening to see India's ancient science become so popular. However, most yoga practitioners have adopted it for good health, as a beauty aid, or for weight loss. That is all very well, but they are unaware of the spiritual depth of the science of *yog*.

The word 'yog' comes from the root *yuj*, which means 'to unite'. Hence, *yog* is 'the state of union'. For example, in Ayurveda, when two medicines are combined, it is called *yog*. In the spiritual context, *yog* refers to the linking of the individual soul with the Supreme Soul. Thus, the ultimate goal of the yogic system is to connect with God. The *Garud Puran* states:

sanyogo yoga ityukto jīvātmaparamātmanoḥ

'The union of the individual consciousness with the Supreme Consciousness is called *yog*.' This happens when our mind is absorbed in the Supreme. And if we do yog along with our karm, it becomes 'Karm yog'.

This was the message of Shree Krishna: 'Always remember Me, and also do your duty of fighting the war.' (Bhagavad Gita 8.7) *tasmāt sarveṣhu kāleṣhu mām anusmara yudhya cha.*

Hence, karm yog literally means:

1) Keep your mind in God (yog), and

2) Do your worldly works (karm) with your body

In karm yog, doing works is nothing new—literally everyone performs worldly duties. The problem is that our mind does not stay in yog. We harbour a variety of emotions, such as stress, fear, grief, frustration, and so on. To become a karm yogi, we must change this: keep the mind yoked to the Supreme and also do our work. In simple parlance, this means 'mind in God, body in the world'.

Again, people do remember God for a little time, but then they forget Him and become engrossed in their worldly duties. Karm yog is the state where the mind continues to remain in the Supreme at all times.

How to remember God all the time. Presently, we are aware of ourselves, 'I am'. Throughout the day, we perceive, 'I am happy', 'I am sad', 'I am hungry', 'I am full', and so on. But we fail to realize 'God is also with me'.

In fact, the Supreme always accompanies us wherever we go. The *Brahmopanishad* states: 'There is one God. He hides in the heart of all beings.' (verse 16) *aeko devaḥ sarvabhūteṣhu gūḍhaḥ*.

We must now add this perception to our consciousness: 'I am not alone. My Lord is always with me as my Witness and my Protector.' This will come by practising to feel the presence of God with us at all times. For example, when you arrive at the office, before starting your work, think, 'Shree Krishna is in front of me. He is watching me. I must do all my works for His pleasure.' Then, every work we perform will become an offering to Him.

Thus, in karm yog, we do not divide our activities, thinking, 'This work is for me, and this is for my Lord.' Instead, since the mind is always absorbed in God, every activity becomes an offering at the altar of the Supreme. And the consequence of the mind's loving remembrance of the Lord is that one attains the eternal realm.

For the Scholars

The first mantra of the *Ishopanishad* declared that the world is pervaded by God. This established beyond doubt that the world is not *mithya*. Does this mean that, like God, the world is also *satya*?

No, if material creation was *satya*, then as per the Bhagavad Gita's statement, 'That which is *satya* never ceases to exist.' (2.16) The *sat* world would then have continued to exist forever.

Now we know very well that there will be pralaya, and creation will cease one day. This means the world is *asat,* meaning 'temporary'. Likewise, everything in this world is also temporary, and hence, the epithet *vināśham* applies to it.

Having explained the art of karm yog, which is essentially karm plus bhakti, the Upanishad now goes even deeper into bhakti. The following mantra prays for a vision of the personal form of God, which is covered by effulgent light. In this way, it expresses preference of worship of the Personal Form of God over the Formless Absolute.

Mantra 15

हिरण्मयेन पात्रेण सत्यस्यापिहितं मुखम् ।
तत्त्वं पूषन्नपावृणु सत्यधर्माय दृष्टये ॥ १५॥

hiraṇmayena pātreṇa satyasyāpihitam mukham
tattvam pūṣhannapāvṛiṇu satyadharmāya dṛiṣhṭaye

hiraṇmayena—by a golden effulgence; *pātreṇa*—covered by; *satyasya*—of the Absolute Truth; *apihitam*—covered; *mukham*—the face; *tat*—that covering; *tvam*—yourself; *pūṣhan*—one who nourishes; *apāvṛiṇu*—kindly remove; *satya*—eternal; *dharmāya*—dharma; *dṛiṣhṭaye*—for beholding.

O Absolute Truth, Who are the Nourisher of devotional rasas! Your divine face is covered by a golden effulgence.

Desirous of following real dharma (which is devotion to You), I pray that You remove the veil of radiance that covers Your Personality, so that I may behold the vision of Your divine form.

This mantra mentions *satya dharma.* Let us understand this phrase first. The Vedic scriptures strongly urge humans to follow dharma. They go to the extent of stating that without dharma, humans are no different from animals. The *Hitopadesh* states:

āhāra nidrā bhaya maithunam cha
sāmānyametat paśhubhirnarāṇām
dharmo hi teṣhāmadhiko viśheṣhaḥ
dharmeṇa hīnāḥ paśhubhiḥ samānāḥ (verse 25)

'Eating, sleeping, fearing, and mating—these activities are common to humans and animals alike. Special to humans is the ability to follow dharma; without it, they are not unlike animals.'

Manu, the ancient lawmaker, said:

- 'If dharma is destroyed, then humanity will be destroyed.' *dharma aeva hato hanti.*
- 'If dharma is followed, then humanity will be protected.' *dharmo rakṣhati rakṣhitaḥ.* (*Manu Smriti*)

The word 'dharma' comes from the root word *dhṛiya,* which means *dhāraṇ karane yogya,* or 'that which is worthy of adopting and upholding'. It includes the actions, values, beliefs, and duties that are appropriate for us.

In Hinduism, dharma is divided into two primary categories: material duties and spiritual duties. Both are essential for a balanced and harmonious life as they serve different purposes.

Material duties (*apara dharma*). This relates to our worldly responsibilities. When we identify ourselves with the body, we have obligations towards our family, society, and nation. Performing these duties is essential for social harmony and order, but they do not suffice for achieving God-realization.

Since *apara dharma* is based on bodily designations, which are transient, it can also be called *asat dharma,* or 'impermanent duties'.

Spiritual duty (*para dharma*). This is our duty towards the Creator, which is to love and serve Him. It is the highest and ultimate duty of the soul. The Shreemad Bhagavatam emphasizes:

> *sa vai pumsām paro dharmo yato bhaktiradhokṣhaje*
> *ahaitukyapratihatā yayātmā suprasīdati* (1.2.6)

'The highest dharma for human beings is bhakti to the Supreme Divine Personality. Such bhakti should be selfless and uninterrupted, for only then will one's soul be satiated.'

The Shreemad Bhagavatam again says: 'On following the principles of dharma, if the hankering to hear blissful loving pastimes of the Creator of the world does not arise in the heart, then such religious observances are mere exertion.' (1.2.8)

The clear import is that the supreme goal of dharma is to have ever-increasing bhakti towards God's names, forms, virtues, pastimes, abodes, and saints. It is also called *satya dharma*, or 'permanent duty'. (Here the meaning of the word *satya* comes from the root *sat*, which means eternal.)

Devotional prayer. The *Ishopanishad* mantra now expresses a fervent prayer. It supplicates God for revealing a vision of His divine form. The word *mukham* refers to God's radiant face. If, as the jnanis claim, God were only *nirgun, nirvishesh, nirakar* (without qualities, attributes, form), then would He have a face? Why would the mantra teach us ever-increasing hankering for a vision of God's radiant face?

It connotes that the personal form of God is the most prized sight for a jiva to behold. It appears as if the devotee has drowned in the mellows of devotion and is earnestly beseeching to behold God's divine form adorned with a gentle smile.

The devotee here says: *hiraṇmayena pātreṇa*, meaning 'O God Who have shrouded Yourself in a veil of light, we are unable to see Your divine form, just as an object in a golden plate is rendered invisible by its sheen and glimmer.'

Here, by means of this allegory, a great philosophical truth is revealed to us. The divine vision of God's personal form is preferred over the splendid vision of His effulgent *Brahmajyoti*. Regarding the *Brahmajyoti*, the *Chaitanya Charitamrit* shares the same spiritual insight:

brahma angakānti tānra nirviśheṣha prakāśhe
sūrya yena charma-chakṣhe jyotirmaya bhāse

(*Madhya Leela* 20.159)

Chaitanya Mahaprabhu explains that when we see the sun with our human eyes, we simply perceive its effulgence but cannot see the details of its abode. Likewise, the *Brahmajyoti*, being worshipped by the jnanis, is nothing but the bodily glow of the Supreme Brahman.

Pūṣhan. In the mantra, the devotee calls God as *Pūṣhan*. This Vedic word is a very intriguing name for God. It refers to One Who is full of nourishing rasa, the transcendental mellows of bliss. Thus, the Vedas also refer to God as 'Rasa'.

raso vai saḥ (*Taittiriya Upanishad* 2.7.1)

'That Supreme Being is of the form of Rasa.'

Do note that this mantra does not say, 'God is full of rasa'. It states that He is rasa Himself. The same mantra of the *Taittiriya Upanishad* continues to say: *rasam hyevāyam labdhvānandī bhavati* 'By attaining God, the soul becomes *rasamaya* (blissful).'

Rasiks are devotees who relish the divine rasa of God. Since He imparts them such nectar, He is called *Pūṣhan*.

Nourished with an array of devotional sentiments, the soul then lovingly serves God. Such devotional service is satisfying to the Lord. Thus, the name *Pūṣhan* applies to Him also, as 'the One who gets nourished by the soul's love'.

The rasik saints, in their loving manner, refer to this *Pūṣhan Brahman* as *Rasik Shiromani* (Crest-Jewel of Rasiks), *Madhuradipati* (the Lord of all-sweetness), *Rasaraj* (the King of Rasa), and so on.

In summary, this Veda mantra instructs us to go beyond God's effulgent *Brahmajyoti* aspect. It inspires us to increase our thirst for beholding His *rasamaya* form. It guides us to desire a vision of His radiant face endowed with a gentle smile that is full of sweetness. Doing so will give the highest fulfillment to our soul.

For the Scholars

The mantra conveys that our *satya dharma* is bhakti—loving devotion to God. Only by bhakti can one behold a vision of the Supreme (*driśhtaye*). *Asat dharma* is insufficient for getting darshan of God. Leaving no doubt in the matter, the Bhagavad Gita states:

bhaktyā tv ananyayā śhakya aham evam-vidho 'rjuna
jñātum draṣhṭum cha tattvena praveṣhṭum cha parantapa

(verse 11.54)

'O Arjun, by unalloyed devotion alone can I be known as I am, standing before you. Thereby, on receiving My divine vision, O scorcher of foes, one can enter into union with Me.'

There is much confusion regarding true dharma. Even in the congregation of holy people, differing perspectives are presented. Some hold *tapasya* (austerities) to be the highest dharma, others consider *daan* (donation) as the supreme activity. Then, there are those who espouse the virtues of *paropakar* (altruism), while others vote for *vrata* (fasting). Some hold *puja-path* (ritualistic worship) as the highest, and yet others promote the performance of yajnas (fire sacrifices) as the highest. Some are proponents of *yam-niyam* (adherence to do's and don'ts from the scriptures).

While all these are good activities and pious deeds, without bhakti, they do not suffice for attaining God. The para dharma, *satya dharma*, highest dharma, or true dharma is bhakti to the Supreme Divine Personality. Let us see what the scriptures say in this regard.

The Shreemad Bhagavatam states:

dharmaḥ satyadayopeto vidya vā tapasānvitā
madbhaktyāpetamātmānam na samyak prapunāti hi
(verse 11.14.22)

'Dharma that is conjoined with truth and mercy is considered the highest material dharma. *Tapasya* endowed with knowledge is considered the highest austerity. But without devotion to Me, even such lofty dharma and *tapasya* cannot purify the consciousness of the jiva.'

The *Mundakopanishad* states:

dhanugṛihītvaupaniṣhadam mahāstram
śharam hyupāsāniśhitam sandhayīta
āyamya tadbhāvagatena chetasā lakṣhyam
tadevākṣharam somya viddhi (2.2.3)

'Take the bow of Upanishadic wisdom. On this great weapon, place the arrow of bhakti. Let bhav be the razor edge of the arrow. Then, go and hunt for the Supreme Brahman.'

The *Shwetashvatar Upanishad* states:

yasya deve parā bhaktiryathā deve tathā gurau
tasyaite kathitā hyarthāḥ prakāśhante mahātmanaḥ

'Those who are engaged in bhakti to the Supreme and maintain a similar bhav towards their guru, to such great souls the import of the Vedas is directly revealed in their heart, by the grace of God.'

Shree Krishna affirms the same in the Bhagavad Gita:

nāham vedair na tapasā na dānena na chejyayā
śhakya evam-vidho draṣhṭum dṛiṣhṭavān asi mām yathā
(verse 11.53)

'Neither by the study of the Vedas, nor by penance, charity, or fire sacrifices, can I be seen as you have seen Me.'

The Bhagavad Gita again states:

puruṣhaḥ sa paraḥ pārtha bhaktyā labhyas tvananyayā
yasyāntaḥ-sthāni bhūtāni yena sarvam idam tatam (8.22)

'The Supreme Divine Personality is greater than all that exists. Although He is all-pervading and all living beings are situated in Him, yet He can be known only through devotion.'

In reality, what to say of God-realization, even the purification of one's heart is not possible without bhakti. The Shreemad Bhagavatam states:

katham vinā romaharṣham dravatā chetasā vinā
vinā ' 'nandāśhrukalayā śhudhyed bhaktyā vinā ' 'śhayaḥ
(verse 11.14.23)

'There is no hope for purification of one's heart, until one's devotion ripens to create joy in every pore of the body, the *chitta* melts and is overcome with joy, and tears of bliss roll down the eyes.'

Adi Sankaracharya has also accepted this in the *Prabodh Sudhakar*:

śhuddhyati hi nāntarātmā kṛiṣhṇapadāmbhoja
bhaktimṛite (verse 167)

'Without having tasted the nectar of devotion to the lotus feet of Shree Krishna, the *antaḥ-karaṇ* (heart) can never be purified.'

As above, there are thousands of verses in the scriptures stating that God-realization requires bhakti. But for the purpose of explaining the mantra, let these suffice here. Nevertheless, the point conclusively proved—on the basis of the scriptures—is that *para dharma* (*satya dharma*) is selfless uninterrupted devotion to the Supreme Divine Personality.

Having expressed the desire to see the personal form of God, the devotee's yearning for darshan grows. So, in the next mantra he repeats the prayer with greater intensity, for a vision of the Supreme Divine Personality.

Mantra 16

पूषन्नेकर्षे यम सूर्य प्राजापत्य
व्यूह रश्मीन् समूह तेजो ।
यत्ते रूपं कल्याणतमं तत्ते पश्यामि
योऽसावसौ पुरुषः सोऽहमस्मि ॥ १६॥

pūṣhannaekarṣhe yama sūrya prājāpatya
vyūha raśhmīn samūha tejo
yatte rūpam kalyāṇatamam tatte paśhyāmi
yo 'sāvasau puruṣhaḥ so 'hamasmi

pūṣhan—nourisher of devotional sentiments; *aekarṣhe*—highest rishi, knower of the Vedas; *yama*—regulator; *sūrya*—sun, inspirer of the souls; *prājāpatya*—the giver of joy to Brahma; *vyūha*—please remove; *raśhmīn*—brilliant rays; *samūha*—please withdraw; *tejaḥ*—divine effulgence; *yat*—so that; *te*—your; *rūpam*—form; *kalyāṇa-tamam*—most auspicious; *tat*—that; *te*—your; *paśhyāmi*—I may see; *yaḥ*—one who is; *asau*—like the sun; *asau*—that; *puruṣhaḥ*—Supreme Personality; *saḥ*—myself; *aham*—I; *asmi*—am.

O Nourisher of devotional sentiments! O Supreme Knower of the Vedas! O Regulator of all! O Inspirer of the souls! O Giver of joy to Brahma! Please remove these brilliant rays and withdraw this divine effulgence, so that I may behold the vision of Your most auspicious Form. Being a fragmental part of the Supreme, I am one with You.

In this mantra, the worshipper again prays to receive darshan of the most blissful form of God. He clarifies that he hankers for His personal form, which nourishes the transcendental mellows of devotion, and not the form that is of the nature of a brilliant light.

The devotee expresses his sentiment, using a variety of names of God, each of which bears a deep and different meaning. They are: *Pūṣhan*, *Aekarṣhi*, *Yama*, *Sūrya*, and *Prājāpatya*.

At first glance, these appear to be the names of celestial gods in the material realm, which is why some scholars have mistakenly concluded that the devotee is praying to the devatas. However, bear in mind this verse is a continuation of the prayer from the previous mantra, addressed to the Supreme Brahman and not to the celestial gods. Thus, these names here refer to the Supreme Divine Personality.

Before unravelling the secrets of these names, it is important to note that word meanings of Vedic mantras differ as per the context. This is why the *Brahma Sutra* cautions us: *prakaraṇāchcha* (1.2.10) 'Understand the meanings of words in the scriptures with reference to their context.'

So, now, we must comprehend these five names—*Pūṣhan*, *Aekarṣhi*, *Yama*, *Sūrya*, and *Prājāpatya*—in their relationship to God.

Pūṣhan. We came across this word in the 15th mantra and analyzed its meaning. Let us go deeper now. The word *Pūṣhan* is made of the root *pūṣh* and the suffix *kanin*. The literal meaning is *poṣhita karane vālā*, 'one who nourishes' or 'one who provides the juice that nourishes life'.

So, now those who maintain and nourish vegetation are also known as Pusha. From a transcendental perspective, God is *Pusha*, meaning 'the One who nourishes His devotees with transcendental mellows of devotion'. This, He does with two aspects of His nature:

1. *Madhu svabhav*. As the Ocean of bliss, God directly bestows nectar-like bliss in the heart of His purified devotees. Such devotees forever remain absorbed in this sweet rasa.

2. *Madhukar svabhav*. Just as we experience the pleasures of the material world through our senses, God experiences divine rasa through the souls. Residing in His devotees' hearts, God tastes the sweetness of their devotional sentiments and relishes sweet rasa for Himself.

In this manner, the Nourisher of His devotees, God, is referred to here as *Pūṣhan.*

Aekarṣhi. God is referred to as *Aekarṣhi*, conveying the idea that He is *aekamātra ṛiṣhi* or 'the sole rishi'. How can He be the sole rishi? Let us understand the meaning of *ṛiṣhi* in depth. As per Sanskrit:

ṛiṣhati prāpnoti sarvān mantrān jñānena
paśhyati sansāra pāram vā

'He who has obtained *ṛit* i.e. practical realization of the knowledge in the mantras, and who sees both the gross and subtle worlds, is known as a rishi.'

Every Vedic mantra has a *mantra-draṣhtā ṛiṣhi* i.e. the sage who has completely realized the meaning of that particular mantra. However, no sage can claim to have mastered the meaning of every mantra. God alone understands all the Vedas. Thus, He is the singular highest rishi, or the *Aekarṣhi.*

Yama. Etymologically speaking, its root is *yamu bandhane,* which literally means 'one who binds and controls'. At the time of death, Yamraj, the god of death, binds the jiva with His *yama-pāśha* (snare) and forcibly drags it out of the body.

In the context of this mantra, the devotee has three main motives to address God as *Yama.* First, Yamraj appears at the time of a living being's death and administers his judgement on the sins and pious deeds of the jiva. Likewise, at the time of God-realization, God appears in front of His devotee as the *ātyantikmṛityu* 'the last death'. After this, the devotee is forever free from the cycle of birth and death. Further, for the surrendered soul, God destroys the unlimited sins and pious deeds of the devotee. Thus, He is the greatest *Yamadeva.*

The second motive is to recognize that creation is under God's absolute control. It manifests by His wish, is maintained by His powers, and is dissolved when He wants. Thus, God is the biggest binder and controller, and therefore, the greatest *Yama.*

The third motive is that the Lord binds the soul in an appropriate *yoni* (species), based upon the jiva's actions and qualities. God accomplishes this extremely subtle work of bondage and control with great ease, being the In-dweller in everyone's heart. Thus, He is the biggest *Yama Niyāmak* (one who enforces the principle).

Prājāpatya. Generally the word *prajāpati* refers to 'ancestor'. So, *prājāpatya* would mean 'head of *Prajāpati Lok* (abode of *Prajāpatis*)'. But in reference to the context, *prajāpati* indicates the 'head ancestor of all species in the universe, including the *prajāpatis* themselves'. This is the first *prajāpati* (foremost father of all species), Shree Brahma.

In the present context, *Prājāpatya* carries three meanings. The first import is 'that which is dear to *Prajāpati Brahma*'. It is well known that Shree Brahma sits in his abode, which is *Satya Lok,* and remains absorbed in meditation on God. Brahma's prayer, the *Brahma Samhita,* is a testament to how deeply He loves Shree Krishna. Hence, *Prājāpatya* means 'that God who is immensely loved by Shree Brahma'.

The second meaning of *Prājāpatya* is *prajāpatinandan.* Shree Krishna is known as *Nandanandan* because He gives *anand* to Nand Baba. Likewise, God is *Prajāpatinandan* i.e. 'the One Who bestows divine bliss to *Prajāpati Brahma*'.

It is almost as if the devotee is saying, 'O Lord, the way You bestow bliss to Shree Brahma, similarly, You are my sole cause of joy as well. Please bless me with the vision of Your divine form and imbue me with that divine joy.'

The third meaning of *Prājāpatya* is: 'He who Resides within all *prajā* (living beings) of creation, as their indwelling Lord and Master.' Jagadguru Ramanujacharya has accepted this definition of *Prājāpatya.*

Sūrya. When the suffix *kyap* is added to the root *sṛvi*, the word *sūrya* is obtained. Etymologically: *suvati karmaṇi lokam prerayati iti sūryaḥ* '*Sūrya* is the one whose presence inspires the living entities in the world to act.'

We experience this definition of *Sūrya* every day. Every sunrise refreshes the world with renewed energy and vanquishes our tamasic slumber. We become inspired to engage in our day-to-day actions. Similarly, God empowers all living entities to do their works. By the power of God, the body-senses-mind-intellect become operational. Thus, He is aptly referred to as *Sūrya*, or 'the One Who inspires jivas to act'.

The name also conveys a devotional mellow of bhakti, 'O Resplendent *Sūrya*! By Your mere presence, I am now inspired to serve You. Therefore, please withdraw this shining veil that covers Your sweet personal form. Bless me so that I may behold Thee! Please accept me.'

With profuse love, he speaks to God, 'O Lord! Your most munificent form, the vision of which millions of yogis hanker for, is available only to those whom You grace. Please grant me a vision of the *sat-chit-anand* form of the Supreme Purush!'

The devotee concludes by exclaiming: *so 'hamasmi* 'I am one with You.' This oneness does not mean that the devotee has realized he is God, else why would he continue praying? Rather, the statement is made in the spirit of union.

The oneness of creation with its Creator is extensively reiterated in the Upanishads. The *Brihadaranyak Upanishad* states: *aekākī na ramate* (1.4.3) 'At the beginning of creation, that Supreme Brahman was alone. However, He did not like solitude.'

Likewise, the *Taittiriya Upanishad* says: *so 'kāmayata. Bahu syām prajāyeyeti* (2.6.1) 'He desired to become diverse in the form of numerous living entities.'

Again, the *Katha Upanishad* reiterates: *aeko vaśhī sarvabhutāntarātmā aekam rūpam bahudhā yaḥ karoti* (2.2.12) 'Pervading all sentient-insentient creation, He is the sole controller operating from within everyone. He divides His single form into multitudes of forms at the time of creation.'

All the above mantras from the Upanishads indicate that the One became many. Hence, between the soul and God, there is simultaneous oneness and duality. Chaitanya Mahaprabhu explained this as *Achintya Bhedabhed*, Ramanujacharya explained it as *Vishishta Advaita*, Nimbarkacharya explained it as *Dvaita Advaita*, and Vallabhacharya propounded it as *Shuddha Advaita*.

Thus, the mantra is not a clarion call for merging into God, instead it inspires us to make service to God with loving devotional sentiments, our ultimate goal. This is the highest goal of the jiva. In the next mantra, the Upanishad describes the devotee's prayer to God to grant him eternal service in God's *nitya leela* (eternal pastimes) in the divine abode.

For the Scholars

These last three verses of the *Ishopanishad* express enhanced devotional sentiments. Some commentators, who do not realize the value of devotion in spirituality, have dismissed them as merely 'a dying man's prayers' that have been added at the end. Such a conclusion does injustice to their esoteric devotional significance. Swami Vivekananda writes:

> Sometimes it has been urged without any grounds whatsoever that there is no ideal of bhakti in the Upanishads. Those who have been students of the Upanishads know that this is not true. There is enough of bhakti in every Upanishad if you will only seek for it.[15]

Shree Aurobindo, in his commentary on the *Ishopanishad*, also touches upon the problem of understanding the Vedas in a limited context:

> An European or his disciple in scholarship can no more enter into the spirit of the Veda than the wind can blow freely in a closed room. And pedants especially can never go beyond the manipulation of words. Men like Max Müller presume to lecture us on our Veda and Vedanta because they know something of Sanscrit grammar; but when we come to them for light, we find them playing marbles on the doorsteps of the outer court of the temple.[16]

Swami Chinmayananda also disagrees with the interpretation that the verses are 'a dying man's prayer'. He states, in his commentary on the *Ishopanishad*:

---

[15] 'Complete Works of Swami Vivekananda, Vol. III, Lectures from Colombo to Almora, Vedanta in its Application to Indian Life', *Essential Books of Ramakrishna Order*, https://englishbooks.rkmm.org/s/tsv/m/the-complete-works-of-swami-vivekananda/a/3-4-12-vedānta-in-its-application-to-indian-life. Last accessed on 15 March 2025.

[16] Sri Aurobindo, *Isha Upanishad*, Sri Aurobindo Ashram Trust, Pondicherry, 2003, p. 133.

> ...the great seer of the Upanishad is indirectly pointing out to the seeker that, during the period of sadhana, every seeker of Vedanta must necessarily have, as an important item of his sadhana an unflinching, deep, and ardent devotion for a personal God.[17]

Metaphorical tools used in Vedas. To highlight an attribute, the Vedas often employ metaphorical constructions. Whenever the Supreme manifests any of His divine attributes in exceptional measure, He is addressed by names, such as Agni, Prajapati, Indra, and so on. This is done to increase the mutual rasa of both the worshipper and the Worshipped.

The *Manu Smriti* states:

aetameke vadantyagnim manumanye prajāpatim
indrameke pare prāṇamapare brahma śhāśhvatam

(verse 12/123)

'That Supreme Everlasting Entity is one. However, some refer to Him as Agni, some as Prajapati, some as Indra, some as Prana, and some call Him Brahma.'

Until now, the devotee's prayer was for divine darshan of God's personal form. Now he wants to selflessly serve His Lord in the divine abode. To fulfill this aspiration, he seeks to offer the highest sacrifice. Through a heart-touching prayer, he urges God to accept the offering of his very life force.

---

17 Chinmayananda, Swami, *Isavasya Upanisad: God in and as everything*, Central Chinmaya Mission Trust, Mumbai, 2013, Kindle e-book.

Mantra 17

वायुरनिलममृतमथेदं भस्मान्तं शरीरम् ।
ॐ क्रतो स्मर कृतं स्मर क्रतो स्मर कृतं स्मर ॥ १७॥

vāyuranilam amṛitamathedam bhasmāntam śharīram
oṁ krato smara kṛitam smara krato smara kṛitam smara

vāyuḥ—life airs; *anilam*—one who is the basis of the life force; *amṛitam*—bestower of nectar; *atha*—now; *idam*—this; *bhasmāntam*—become holy ash; *śharīram*—body; *oṁ*—sacred syllable representing the formless aspect of God; *krato*—enjoyer of sacrifices; *smara*—remember; *kṛitam*—everything done by me; *smara*—remember; *krato*—enjoyer of sacrifices; *smara*—remember; *kṛitam*—all my acts of devotion; *smara*—remember.

May my prana now merge into my *Pranadhar,* Who is the Bestower of nectar-like sweetness. May this body burn in the fire of devotion and become holy ash. Om! O Enjoyer of my bhakti yajna! To You, I dedicate all my devotional efforts. Please remember me (grace me), Your devotee. I offer my all to You. Please remember to consummate my deepest aspiration.

A materially bound soul does not choose its next birth; God decides on the basis of one's karma and consciousness. But here, the devotee—in a gush of devotional sentiments—prays to be elevated to the divine abode and enter the *nitya leela* of God.

Since sentiments expressed in the mantra are deeply devotional, some scholars have completely missed the spirit of this mantra.

To establish its true meaning, beyond doubt, I request the kind reader's permission to go deeper in this mantra, minutely inspecting its words, to grasp their real import.

Vāyuḥ. The life airs in the body are referred to as *vāyuḥ*, meaning 'air', or *prana*. These five-fold prana are: *pāna*, *apāna*, *samāna*, *udāna*, and *vyāna*. They are together called *pancha-prana*, or simply *prana*. The prana energizes various biological functions in the body, enabling our limbs and organs to function.

In this mantra, however, the devotee is praying to God to dissolve his prana! This sentiment can be understood in the context of the devotee's increasing thirst for God's love. In the *viraha bhav* of longing for the Supreme, there comes a point when life seems pointless without meeting the Lord.

Chaitanya Mahaprabhu expresses this kind of sentiment: *śhūnyāyitam jagat sarvam govinda viraheṇa me* 'O Shree Krishna! In the mood of separation from You, the entire cosmos seems pointless and void to me.' (*Shikshashtakam* 7)

Here, the devotee has understood that the highest goal of the jiva is to attain God's love and serve Him selflessly in His *nitya leela*. Thus, to obtain the cherished goal, the devotee prays fervently. Presently, his body and life airs are still material. These two hinder him from attaining a divine body for serving his Lord. Thus, in this mantra, the devotee prays to God to help him get rid of both these obstacles. He says, 'Please dissolve my life airs into *anilam*.'

Anilam. The devotee uses this special word, *anilam*. Its simple meaning is 'totality of air'. However, here it has a very special connotation. As per the *Nirukta* Sanskrit dictionary: *an iti* *jīvati anena*. The root *an* in *anil* means '**that from which others obtain life**'.

By employing the word *anilam*, the devotee is expressing the *bhav* that God is the basis of his life, and thus, his *Pranadhar*.

Amṛitam. The devotee also refers to God as *amṛitam.* One meaning of *amṛit* is immortal, or devoid of death. A second meaning of *amṛit* is 'bestower of nectar-like sweetness'. This meaning is more relevant to the mantra.

The *rasamaya* form of God is called ***Amrit*** in the Vedas. We souls are tiny fragments of that ***amrit*** God. The *Shwetashvatar Upanishad* states: *amṛitasya putrāḥ* (2.5) 'All jivas are children of the ***amrit*** God, Who is an Ocean of nectar-like sweetness.'

The devotee's prayer thus seems to say, 'O Lord, Who are the Bestower of nectar-like sweetness! You alone are my *Pranadhar* (basis of my life force). So, please absorb my prana into Yourself.'

With this sentiment, the devotee wishes to offer the sacrifice of dissolving his life force into God. The desire to serve his Lord has taken such a pitch that the devotee happily proclaims: *idam śharīram bhasmāntam* 'O Lord of my prana! Please render this body to ashes.'

This is a natural and spontaneous loving utterance from the devotee in the highest pitch of devotion. He is experiencing *virahāgni*, i.e. 'fire-like intense longing' for God. The fire of devotion that appears in a devotee's heart has the capacity to burn to ashes the five sheaths that cover the soul. These are *pancha koshas—annamaya kosha* (gross sheath), *pranamaya kosha* (vital energy sheath), *manomaya kosha* (mental sheath), *vijnanamaya kosha* (intellectual sheath), and *anandmaya kosha* (bliss sheath).

For the soul to get liberated, all these five sheaths need to be destroyed. On the path of Hatha Yog, sadhaks do *panchagni kriya* and other austerities to burn these sheaths. However, on the path of bhakti, there is a simple solution. Maharshi Kapil explains: '*Nishkām* bhakti is so powerful, that it naturally burns the five *koshas* enveloping the soul, just as the fire of digestion burns all we eat.' (Bhagavatam 3.25.33) *animittā bhāgavatī bhaktiḥ siddhergarīyasī, jarayatyāśhu yā kośham nigīrṇamanalo yathā.*

Thus, the prayer expresses the devotee's desire to transform the body to holy ash in the fire of devotion. Devotees frequently harbour the desire to sacrifice their all on the incomparably beautiful form of the Lord. When Vibheeshan saw Shree Ram, the Reservoir of all beauty, he was awestruck and dumbfounded so much so that he even forgot to blink and kept beholding God's divine form. *Bahuri rāma chhabidhāma bilokī, raheu ṭhaṭuki ekaṭaka pala rokī* (*Ramcharitmanas Sundar Kand* 5.44.2). The same sentiment is being echoed in this *Ishopanishad* mantra.

Atha. This word further enhances the expression of devotion. Usually *atha* conveys *ab*, meaning 'after these events'.

Here, the sentiment expressed is, 'O Lord! My thirst for Your love has increased so much that my life force can leave any moment now. Thus, please accept my request and make me Yours.'

We have seen how, in the first line of the mantra, the devotee prays to God with great fervour. Now, come to the second line of this prayerful verse. To understand its import, we must comprehend the two powerful words used.

Krataḥ (O Enjoyer of sacrifices). In Vedic terminology, the enjoyer of sacrifices is referred to as *krataḥ*. Factually, the aim of all ritualistic sacrifices is to please God. Hence, He is the ultimate *Krataḥ*, or 'Yajna Purush'.

Krataḥ is also 'one who appears at the end of the yajna performance and accepts the offering'. From this perspective as well, God is the *Yajna Purush.*

In karm-kand, there are various kinds of yajnas, such as *pitṛi-kriya, agnihotra, aśhvamedha yajna,* and so on. In upasana-kand, the yajna is bhakti. Shree Krishna states: 'Of all the yajnas, I am the chanting of My holy names.' (Gita 10.25)

Hence, for the sacrifice of devotion, the Lord is the *Yajna Purush.* This is why, here God is called *Krataḥ.*

***Kṛitam* or 'devotional offerings'.** The devotee says, 'Please remember me, Your devotee. Please remember my *kṛitam.* I properly utilized *vidya* and *avidya.* I made judicious use of *sambhūti* and *asambhūti.* Now I wish to do *atma-samarpan,* offer my very self to You. Please remember my karma and I. Further, as You wish.'

When the *Yajna Purush* appears, one prayerfully asks to be bestowed the fruit of the yajna. Here too, God, as the *Yajna Purush,* is being asked to grant the boon of divine service in the divine abode.

Krato smara kṛitam smara. This prayer is repeated twice in the second line of the mantra. The reader may wonder, what is the need for it? Is it necessary to remind God of anything? Is God forgetful that He needs to be told how much penance and sadhana a jiva has rendered?

This question is appropriate since the Supreme is He Who knows every thought, intention, and action of the jiva. Without being aware, how would He bestow the fruit of our karmas? Furthermore, in the *Varaha Puran*, the Lord Himself says:

vātādi doṣheṇa madbhaktom mām na cha smaret
aham smarāmi madbhaktam nayāmi paramām gatim

'Having remembered Me for all his life, if My pure devotee is not able to remember Me at the time of death, owing to *vāta* and other defects, then I remember My devotee and lead him to the highest destination.'

Hence, there is no question of God forgetting the devotee. Besides, He does not need to be reminded because of a memory defect. The reason for the prayer is that it is a spontaneous utterance of devotion. All devotees have offered prayers to the Lord, knowing fully well that He already knows their heart. Besides, the prayer becomes a means of crystallizing the devotees' thoughts and training the mind to harbour the proper sentiments.

It is also an expression that is pleasing to God. Thus, in the mantra, the devotee repeats the entreaty: *krato smara kṛitam smara, krato smara kṛitam smara*, meaning 'O Enjoyer of my bhakti yajna! To You I dedicate all my devotional efforts. Please remember me (grace me), Your devotee. I offer my all to You. Please remember to consummate my deepest aspiration.'

Here, the devotee wants to make the highest offering in his

devotional penance—that of his own life force. He is filled with firm conviction that God will remove the obstacles in his entry to the divine abode and accept him.

Om. The devotee has presented himself for the final journey and made his intent known to God. The *praṇava* Om is employed to portray this readiness. In the Vedic system, the syllable Om is used to invoke auspiciousness before the commencement of any important activity.

Here, the devotee anticipates the event of destroying the body in the fire of devotion and dissolving his life force. Thus, the syllable Om is appropriately invoked at the beginning.

This mantra teaches us that our highest goal should go beyond getting darshan of God's personal form. Rather, we should aim to selflessly serve the Supreme in His divine abode. Until this highest devotional sentiment is developed, spiritual aspirants must keep enhancing their thirst for meeting God and serving Him.

In this mantra, with the deepest sentiments of devotional longing for God, the devotee prayed to sacrifice his very prana upon his Pranadhar. *Now, in the next mantra, he appeals to the Lord's mercy that all impediments preventing his supreme ascension may be burnt. He completes his prayer by beseeching for seva in the divine abode of God.*

Mantra 18

अग्ने नय सुपथा राये अस्मान्
विश्वानि देव वयुनानि विद्वान् ।

युयोध्यस्मज्जुहुराणमेनो
भूयिष्ठां ते नमउक्तिं विधेम ॥ १८॥

agne naya supathā rāye asmān
viśhvāni deva vayunāni vidvān
yuyodhyasmajjuhurāṇameno
bhūyiṣhṭhām te namauktim vidhema

agne—worshippable deity of fire; *naya*—kindly guide; *supathā*—by a divine path; *rāye*—supreme treasure of life; *asmān*—us; *viśhvāni*—all; *deva*—O lord; *vayunāni*—actions; *vidvān*—the knower; *yuyodhi*—please destroy; *asmat*—from us; *juhurāṇam*—all obstacles on the path; *enaḥ*—all defects; *bhūyiṣhṭhām*—over and over again; *te*—unto you; *namaḥ*—offer obesiance; *uktim*—glorify; *vidhema*—I do.

O Lord, Thou art the Deity of the fire of devotion. O Supreme Treasure of life, please take us by the divine path. O Resplendent One! You know all our countless intentions and karma performed in this world of maya. Please destroy the karmas that bind us and prevent us from attaining Your divine abode. We repeatedly sing Your glories and offer our prayerful obeisance unto You.

This mantra is a heartfelt prayer to enter into God's divine abode. It is also found in the *Yajur Veda* (5.36 and 7.43) and *Rig Veda* (1.189.1). As the final mantra of the *Ishopanishad*, it consummates the *tattva jnana* and bhakti of the previous mantras. It thus takes us on a sublime devotional flight.

To get an insight into its deeply spiritual meaning, we must begin by comprehending the two epithets employed: *agni* and *deva*.

Agni. Using the literal meaning of *agni*, some scholars have opined that the devotee is praying to Agni deva, the celestial god of fire. However, in the context of the previous mantras, *Agni*, here, refers to the Supreme Divine Lord.

In the previous mantra, God was addressed as *Krataḥ* to indicate that He is the *Yajna Purush* of the sacrifice of bhakti. To that *Yajna Purush*, the sentiments of longing were expressed. There was no mention of the celestial god of fire. In continuation from mantra 17, the same *Yajna Purush* is now being addressed as *Agni*—the One who ignites the fire of devotion in our heart. In fact, the Vedas refer to God by this name in other places as well:

brahma hī agniḥ (*Shatpath Brahman*)

'God Himself is *Agni*.'

In the present mantra, expressive words, such as *Agni* and *Deva*, are used for God. Since He is the Deity presiding over the devotee's devotional fire, the devotee calls Him as *Agni*. Let us now dissect the second term.

Deva. Etymologically, the word deva connotes *divyatīti devaḥ* 'one who is resplendent from their own brilliance is known as a deva.' Maharshi Yask, the well-known ancient commentator on the Vedas, supports this definition:

devo dānādvā dīpanādvā dyotanādvā (*Nighaṇtu*)

'The residents of heaven who, by their very own nature, are inclined to contribute, to shine, and to illuminate, are known as deva.'

Thus, deva is a personality who is 'resplendent' and 'self-effulgent'. Celestial beings do not have a body like ours which is predominantly composed of earth and water. In contrast, the devatas' body is primarily made of the resplendence of fire, which makes them naturally luminous.

Yet, when compared to the boundless brilliance of God, the radiance of a devata is like the glow of a firefly in front of the sun. Appropriately, thus, God is also *Deva*, the Lord of resplendence. Since the luminosity of the celestials is powered by God, He is in fact *Param Deva*, the *diptīvāna* or 'the Shining One'. The *Shwetashvatar Upanishad* says:

> *aeko devaḥ sarvabhūteṣhu gūḍhaḥ sarvavyāpī*
> *sarvabhūtāntarātmā* (6.11)

'There is only one *Deva*. He pervades all living entities and resides within them as the indwelling Controller.'

Additionally, God's divine form is decorated with various ornaments and clothing. These are made from the divine energy, Yogmaya. The radiance from these—combined with His natural bodily lustre—adds another dimension of divine beauty to God. Since He is endowed with such an effulgence, the devotee calls the Lord as *Deva*. Thus, it has been established that *Agni* and *Deva* are employed as epithets for the Supreme.

Rāye. In the mantra, the devotee uses the word *rāye*, to declare the motive of his prayers to God. It comes from the root *raiḥ*. In Sanskrit, *raiḥ* means 'wealth that is endowed with rays of light'. It is used to refer to jewels, gemstones, gold, and similar radiant forms of wealth. This same radiant wealth is the motive in the mantra.

However, in the current context, the devotee is seeking to sacrifice his all. Given the devotee's exalted surrender, one may wonder what wealth does he cherish? This is resolved when we understand that the devotee considers God as His Supreme Treasure and is therefore praying to attain Him.

From a philosophical perspective, too, God is self-effulgent. Thus, by using *rāyaḥ* in his prayer, the devotee is in effect conveying, 'O Radiant Treasure of my life!'

Viśhvāni-vayunāni-vidvān.

Viśhvāni means 'the set of countless universes in the material realm'. Here it refers to the entirety of creation.

Vayunāni has a rather interesting meaning. The life span of the world is known as *vaya*. The highest limit of creation is known as *vayonādha*. And the science of creation is known as *vayuna*.

Vidvān means 'one endowed with special knowledge'. Here, the devotee is hailing God as a special kind of a scholar.

When combined, *viśhvāni-vayunāni-vidvān* means 'the Scholar who knows all the sciences of all the worlds in creation'.

In the devotee's prayer, the phrase connotes: 'O Lord! You are so knowledgeable that You are the Knower of every science within the ken of creation. Thus, You know of all my sinful deeds. Please destroy all my *yuyodhi* (impious deeds) that keep me from You. Why the delay?'

Juhurāṇam. Etymologically, from the *Shabda-Kalpadrum* Sanskrit dictionary, the word *juhurāṇam* comes from the sutra: *havṛi kautilye*. It means 'questionable deeds performed on an impious path'.

This word includes the *prārabdh* and *kriyamāṇ* karmas of this lifetime and the accumulated *sañchit* karmas of endless lives. Further, it also includes the material *vasanas* (residual desires) and worldly *smritis* (subtle impressions in the memory).

They all are categorized as *juhurāṇam*, irrespective of whether they are moral or immoral—*paap* or *punya*. While *paap* leads us to hell, *punya* leads us to heaven. Both are therefore binding. For God-realization, all residual *paap* and *punya* will need to be burnt.

Thus, the devotee requests: 'O Lord! Whatever garbage binds my *antaḥ-karaṇ* (mind-intellect-ego) to maya, please render *yuyodhi* unto it—please destroy it. Whether it be tamasic, rajasic, or sattvic, I do not wish to remain stuck with any of it. I only wish to be bound in love to You, Who are the Treasure of my life.'

The devotee now offers himself in the fire of separation (*virahāgni*) that arises from his penance of devotion. He expresses it with devotional finesse, saying 'O Lord! I repeatedly sing Your glories and offer my prayerful obeisance unto You. By the true path (***supathā***), please lead us (***naya***) to Your divine abode, so that we may give You happiness for eternity.'

Asmān. Interestingly, the devotee's prayer has now changed to the plural form. Instead of saying *mām* (me), he uses the word *asmān* (us). Thus, he says: *asmān supathā naya* 'Please lead us by the true path.'

Some scholars explain that the devotee is now including his guru in the prayer, and saying, 'Please take us both, guru and disciple.' However, if this were the connotation of the devotee, he would have used *āvām*. Instead, he is saying, *asmān*, which is a second-degree plural of *āvām*. This conveys that besides the guru and disciple, he is now also praying for others.

Further, in the same mantra, the devotee says, 'Please destroy our (*asmat*) sins.' Again, the same question arises. Why does he employ the fifth-degree plural form to indicate many? Are there others as well whose sins are to be destroyed?

This question is resolved by appreciating the devotional sentiments expressed. One whose heart has been purified through bhakti abandons self-centred ways of thinking and starts desiring everyone's welfare. Thus, the devotee is now feeling compassion for other jivas in his proximity. So, he is praying on behalf of all of them: 'O Lord! If you are pleased with me, then heed my request. Please act for the highest benefit of all these jivas under the spell of maya. Along with me, please destroy the sins for all the others.' Thus, he says *asmat juhurāṇam*, instead of *mām juhurāṇam*.

Prahalad Maharaj expressed the same sentiment in his prayers to Bhagavan Nrisingh. He said:

> *naitānvihāya kṛipaṇānvimumukṣha aeko*
> *nānyam tvadasya śharaṇam bhramato 'nupaśhye*
>
> (Bhagavatam 7.9.44)

'Please do not liberate me alone, leaving aside those who are engrossed in maya. Without the shelter of Your lotus feet, they will continue in the cycle of life and death.'

Likewise, Vasudev Dutta prayed to Chaitanya Mahaprabhu (original in Bengali):

> O Lord! I am pained to see the sufferings of the souls under maya. Please transfer their sinful karmas unto me.

I am willing to suffer on their behalf, if it will bring an end to their material life.

—*Chaitanya Charitamrit, Madhya Leela* 15.162–163

With similar sentiments of compassion, the devotee becomes tender hearted and munificent. So, he starts to think of the well-being and fortune of everyone. With this altruistic sentiment and glorifying His Lord again and again, the devotee completes his prayer.

This mantra concludes our journey through the sublime wisdom of the Ishopanishad. *Beginning with the instruction to perceive God everywhere and to do all our work for Him alone, the Upanishad guided us through a balanced path. It synthesizes materialism and spirituality perfectly and inspires us to practise devotion while living in the world. The voyage brought us to the ultimate goal of serving the personal form of God in His divine abode.*

Now, this tiny soul, who is a servant of Jagadguru Shree Kripaluji Maharaj, repeatedly acclaims and salutes the *Ishopanishad's* supramental knowledge and acclaims it as eminently capable of dispelling philosophic confusions and illuminating humanity towards the ultimate welfare.

ॐ पूर्णमदः पूर्णमिदं पूर्णात् पूर्णमुदच्यते ।
पूर्णस्य पूर्णमादाय पूर्णमेवावशिष्यते ॥
ॐ शान्तिः शान्तिः शान्तिः ॥

॥ इत्युपरम्यते ॥

Glossary

abhinivesh	fear of death
Absolute Truth	God
ajnana	ignorance
akarm	work that is done with pure intention, without attachment to results
anandmaya kosha	bliss sheath
annamaya kosha	gross sheath
antaḥ-karaṇ	etheral heart; coloquially referred to as the heart; it consists of the mind, intellect, subconscious mind, and the ego
apara dharma	material duties prescribed in the Vedas, such as those towards family, friends, society, etc.
asmita	ego
asura	demon
atma	soul
atma samarpan	offering one's soul to God
atma-shakti	energy of the soul
Avatar	descension of God or His special powers on earth
avidya	material science
Bhagavan	Supreme Lord, possessor of infinite opulences
bhakti	devotion to God
bhashya	commentary
bhav	sentiment
bhog	material enjoyment
Brahma jnana	knowledge of the Supreme
Brahman	formless aspect of God

deva	celestial god
Dwapar Yug	era that preceded Kali Yug, consisting of 864,000 years
dwesh	hatred
Golok	divine abode of Shree Krishna
gopis	village maidens who resided in Braj when Shree Krishna enacted His pastimes there, about five thousand years ago
gunas	modes of nature
guru	teacher of spirituality
Jagadguru	Spiritual Master of the world; similar to the Pope in Christianity
jiva	tiny soul, a fragment of God
jnana	knowledge
jnana-kand	section of the Vedas explaining spiritual knowledge
jnana shakti	knowledge energy
jnana yog	system of Yog in which emphasis is on knowing the self, which is considered as non-different from God
jnani	1) person of knowledge, 2) one following the path of jnana yog
karm-kand	section of the Vedas explaining ritualistic ceremonies
karm yog	practice of keeping the mind in God as we perform our daily tasks
karm yogi	one who practises karm yog
kriyamāṇ karma	actions we do in the present by our own free will
manomaya kosha	mental sheath
maya	God's material (insentient) energy
mithya	non-existent

Om	the sound that pervades the material universe and can be heard by yogis who tune into it. It is added in the beginning of many Vedic mantras as the seed mantra. It is also a name for the formless aspect of God.
pancha koshas	five sheaths that cover the materially bound soul
paap (pāp)	sin
para dharma	spiritual duty, which is devotion to God
prana	subtle life force energy that pervades the atmosphere, also present in our breath and exists in our body as the five kinds of prana.
pranamaya kosha	vital energy sheath
prārabdh karma	portion of sanchit karmas that we have to face in the present life
punya (puṇya)	good deeds
raga	attachment
rajo guna	mode of passion
sadhak (*sādhak*)	spiritual aspirant
sadhana	spiritual practice
samarpan	dedication of oneself or one's works to God
samsara	cycle of life and death
sañchit karma	all the accumulated karmas that we performed in endless past lives
sansar	world
sat-chit-anand	eternality, sentience, and bliss
sattva guna	mode of goodness
satya	eternal
Satya Lok	abode of Brahma
shakti	energy; power
siddhi	state of perfection; also used for mystical abilities that accrue through yogic sadhana

Supreme Brahman	God
tamo guna	mode of ignorance
tapasya	austerities
upasana	to get close to God
upasana-kand	section of the Vedas discussing devotion and worship
vairagya	detachment
Varnashram dharma	system of prescribed duties in accordance with one's profession and status in life
Vedas	eternal knowledge of God that He manifested at the beginning of creation, and which was passed down from master to disciple through hearing. Sage Ved Vyas divided it into four books—*Rig Veda*, *Yajur Veda*, *Sama Veda*, and *Atharva Veda*.
Vedic scriptures	all the holy texts of Hinduism that accept the authority of the Vedas and elaborate upon them. These include the Vedas, Vedang, Puranas, Itihas, Shad Darshan, Smritis, etc.
vidya	spiritual science
vijnanamaya kosha	intellectual sheath
vikarm	sin
viraha bhav	sentiment of longing for the Supreme
yajna	sacrifice
Yamraj	celestial god of death
yog	1) union with God 2) system that unites the soul with God
Yogmaya	God's bliss-giving energy

Guide to Hindi Pronunciation

Vowels

अ	*a*	as *u* in 'but'
आ	*ā*	as *a* in 'far'
इ	*i*	as *i* in 'pin'
ई	*ī*	as *i* in 'machine'
उ	*u*	as *u* in 'push'
ऊ	*ū*	as *o* in 'move'
ए	*e*	as *a* in 'evade'; when the word starts with ए, use ae
ऐ	*ai*	as *a* in 'mat'; sometimes as *ai* in 'aisle' with the only difference that a should be pronounced as *u* in 'but', not as *a* in 'far'
ओ	*o*	as *o* in 'go'
औ	*au*	as *o* in 'pot' or as *aw* in 'saw'
ऋ	*ṛi*	as *ri* in 'Krishna'[18]
ॠ	*ṛī*	as *ree* in 'spree'

Consonants

Gutturals: Pronounced from the throat

क	*ka*	as *k* in 'kite'
ख	*kha*	as *kh* in 'Eckhart'
ग	*ga*	as *g* in 'goat'

---

[18] Across the many states of India, *ṛi* is pronounced as '*ru*' as *u in* p*u*sh. In most parts of North India, *ṛi* is pronounced as *ri* in K*ri*shna. We have used the North Indian style here.

घ	*gha*	as *gh* in 'dighard'
ङ	*ṅa*	as *n* in 'finger'

Palatals: Pronounced with the middle of the tongue against the palate

च	*cha*	as *ch* in 'channel'
छ	*chha*	as *chh* in 'staunchheart'
ज	*ja*	as *j* in 'jar'
झ	*jha*	as *dgeh* in 'hedgehog'
ञ	*ña*	as *n* in 'lunch'

Cerebrals: Pronounced with the tip of the tongue against the palate

ट	*ṭa*	as *t* in 'tub'
ठ	*ṭha*	as *th* in 'hothead'
ड	*ḍa*	as *d* in 'divine'
ढ	*ḍha*	as *dh* in 'redhead'
ण	*ṇa*	as *n* in 'burnt'

Dentals: Pronounced like the Cerebrals but with the tongue against the teeth

त	*ta*	as *t* in French word 'matron'
थ	*tha*	as *th* in 'ether'
द	*da*	as *th* in 'either'
ध	*dha*	as *dh* in 'Buddha'
न	*na*	as *n* in 'no'

Labials: Pronounced with the lips

प	*pa*	as *p* in 'pink'
फ	*pha*	as *ph* in 'uphill'
ब	*ba*	as *b* in 'boy'

भ	*bha*	as *bh* in 'abhor'
म	*ma*	as *m* in 'man'

Semi-vowels

य	*ya*	as *y* in 'yes'
र	*ra*	as *r* in 'remember'
ल	*la*	as *l* in 'light'
व	*va*	as *v* in 'vine', as *w* in 'swan'

Sibilants

श	*śha*	as *sh* in 'shape'
ष	*ṣha*	as *sh* in 'show'
स	*sa*	as *s* in 'sin'

Aspirate

ह	*ha*	as *h* in 'hut'

Visarga

:	*ḥ*	it is a strong aspirate; also lengthens the preceding vowel and occurs only at the end of a word. It is pronounced as a final *h* sound

Anusvara Nasalized

ं	*m/n*	nasalizes and lengthens the preceding vowel and is pronounced as *n* in the words 'and' or 'anthem'. However, *ṅ* to be used when the anusvara appears at the end of the word
ँ	*ṁ/ṅ*	as *n* in 'gung-ho'

Avagraha

ऽ	'	This is a silent character indicating अ. It is written but not pronounced; used in specific combination (sandhi) rules

Others

क्ष	*kṣha*	as *ksh* in 'freakshow'
ज्ञ	*jña*	as *gy* in 'bigyoung'
ड़	*ṛa*	There is no sign in English to represent the sound ड़. It has been written as *ṛa* but the tip of the tongue quickly flaps down
ढ़	*ṛha*	There is no sign in English to represent the sound ढ़. It has been written as *ṛha* but the tip of the tongue quickly flaps down
श्र	*śhra*	as *śhra* in 'śhravan'
त्र	*tra*	as *tra* in 'mantra'
ज़	*z*	as *z* in 'zaroor'

Index of Verses Quoted

Vedas

chinmātram śhrīharereranśham, Shanti Path Mantra

Atharva Veda

varāheṇa pṛithivī samvidānā, Shanti Path Mantra

Rig Veda

oṁ tryambakam yajāmahe, Shanti Path Mantra
pra tadviṣhṇu stavate, Shanti Path Mantra
ṛite jñānānna muktiḥ, mantra 11
viṣhṇornu kam vīryāṇi, Shanti Path Mantra

Rig Veda, Purush Sooktam

puruṣha aevedam sarvam, mantra 1

Rig Veda, Vishnu Sooktam

yasyoruṣhu triṣhu, Shanti Path Mantra

Shukla Yajur Veda, Shatpath Brahman

brahma hī agniḥ, mantra 18

Upanishads

Atharvashira Upanishad

akṣharāt sanjāyate kālaḥ, mantra 8

Brahmopanishad

aeko devaḥ sarvabhūteṣhu gūḍhaḥ, mantra 14

Brihadaranyak Upanishad

aekākī na ramate, mantra 16
dve vāva brahamaṇo, Shanti Path Mantra

Chhandogya Upanishad

āchāryavān puruṣho hi veda, mantra 13
āhāra śhuddhau sattva śhuddhiḥ, mantra 10
sattvaśhuddhau dhruvā smṛitiḥ, mantra 10

Kathopanishad

uttiṣhṭhata jāgrata prāpya, mantra 2

yaḥ aekaḥ vaśhī, mantra 16

Kenopanishad

iha chedavedīdatha satyamasti, mantra 2

yanmanasā na manute, mantra 8

Maitreyi Upanishad

chittmeva hi sansāraḥ, mantra 13

Mundakopanishad

avidyāyāmantare vartamānāḥ, mantra 9

dhanugṛihītvaupaniṣhadam mahāstram, mantra 15

iṣhtāpūrtam manyamānā variṣhṭham, mantra 2

upāsate puruṣham ye, mantra 8

yathorṇanābhiḥ sṛijate gṛihṇate, mantra 6

Prashnaopanishad

puṇyena punya lokam nayati, mantra 2

Shwetashvatar Upanishad

aeko devaḥ sarvabhūteṣhu, mantra 18

amṛitasya putrāḥ, mantra 17

chetanaśhchetanānām aeko bahūnām, mantra 5

yasya deve parā bhaktiryathā, mantra 15

Taittiriya Upanishad

rasam hyevāyam labdhvānandī, mantra 15

raso vai saḥ, mantra 15

so 'kāmayata, mantra 16

yadāhyevaiṣha aetasminnudaramantaram, mantra 13

Yogshikha Upanishad

sarvajñam sarvagam śhāntam, mantra 4

Vedang

Nirukti - Nighantu

devo dānādvā dīpanādvā, mantra 18

Puranas

Garud Puran

sanyogo yoga ityukto, mantra 14

Harivansh Puran

tvadiyam vastu govind, mantra 1

Kurma Puran

dehadehīvibhedo 'yam neśhvare, mantra 8

Padma Puran

na tasya prākṛitī, mantra 8
yo 'sau nirguṇa, mantra 8

Shreemad Bhagavatam

ahamevāsamevāgre nānyad yat, mantra 1
anādy-avidyā-yuktasya, mantra 13
animittā bhāgavatī bhaktiḥ, mantra 17
dharmaḥ satyadayopeto vidya, mantra 15
katham vinā romaharṣham, mantra 15
naitānvihāya kṛipaṇānvimumukṣha aeko, mantra 18
sa vai pumsām paro, mantra 15
sā vidyā tanmatir yayā, Introduction to the Upanishads
sarvabhūteṣhu yaḥ paśhyed, mantra 7
tene brahma hṛidāya, Introduction to the Upanishads & mantra 8
yatpādapaṅkajaparāganiṣhevatṛiptā, mantra 8
yatpṛithivyām vrīhiyavam hiraṇyam, mantra 3

Skanda Puran

archite devadeveśhe śhankha, mantra 12
guruḥ sākṣhāt parabrahma, mantra 10

Varaha Puran

sarve pūrṇāḥ śhāśhvatāśhcha, Shanti Path Mantra
sarve sarvaguṇaiḥ pūrṇāḥ, Shanti Path Mantra
vatādi doṣheṇa madbhaktom, mantra 17

Vishnu Puran

aiśhvaryasya samagrasya, Shanti Path Mantra
tatkarma yanna bandhāya, mantra 11

Itihas

Bhagavad Gita

aśhochyān-anvaśhochas-tvam, mantra 7
bhaktyā tv ananyayā śhakya, mantra 15
duḥkheṣhv-anudvigna-manāḥ, Shanti Path Mantra
kachchid ajñāna-sammohaḥ, mantra 7
mām cha yo 'vyabhichāreṇa, mantra 13
na hi jñānena sadṛiśham, mantra 11
na mām karmāṇi limpanti, mantra 8
nāham prakāśhaḥ sarvasya, mantra 8
nāham vedair na tapasā, mantra 15
nāsato vidyate bhāvo, mantra 14
naṣhṭo mohaḥ smṛitir, mantra 7
nātyaśhnatastu yogo 'sti, mantra 10
puruṣhaḥ sa paraḥ pārtha, mantra 15
sammohāt smṛiti-vibhramaḥ, mantra 7
samo 'ham sarva-bhūteṣhu, mantra 5
sarvam jñāna-plavenaiva, Introduction to the Upanishads
tad viddhi praṇipātena, mantra 10
tasmāt sarveṣhu kāleṣhu, mantra 14
tri-vidham narakasyedam, mantra 3
vāsudevaḥ sarvamiti, mantra 1
yajña-śhiṣhṭāśhinaḥ santo, mantra 1
yam yam vāpi smaran, mantra 12
yāmimām puṣhpitām vācham, mantra 9
yānti deva-vratā, mantra 12
yasya nāhankṛito bhāvo, mantra 2
yathākāśha-sthito nityam, mantra 4
yo mām paśhyati sarvatra, mantra 6

Maharamayan

bharaṇaḥ poṣhaṇādhāraḥ śharaṇyaḥ, mantra 4

Ramcharitmanas

bahuri rāma chhabidhāma bilokī, mantra 17
chhūṭai mala ki malahi ke dhoeñ, mantra 13
go gochar jahaṅ lagi mana jāī, mantra 4

hima te anala prakaṭa baru hoī, mantra 14
jāken nakha aru jaṭā bisālā, mantra 12
jānata tumhahi tumhai hoi jāī, mantra 7
jo na tarai bhava sāgara, mantra 3
moha sakala byādhinha, mantra 7
nāri muī gṛiha, mantra 9
rāma sindhu ghana, mantra 10
tana binu beda bhajana, mantra 10
samaratha kahuñ nahin, mantra 8
svargau svalpa anta, mantra 12

Shad Darshan

Brahma Sutra
bhoga mātra sāmyalingāchcha, mantra 8
jagad-vyāpāra varjam, mantra 8
prakaraṇāchcha, mantra 16

Mimansa Darshan
svarga kāmo yajeta, mantra 9

Smritis

Manu Smriti
aetmeke vadantyagnim manumanye, mantra 16
bhūtam bhavyam bhaviṣhyam, Introduction to the Upanishads
dharma aeva hato, mantra 15

Other Scriptures

Brahma Samhita
anādirādi govindaḥ sarvakāraṇa, mantra 8
golokanāmni nijadhāmni tale, mantra 4

Chaitanya Charitamrit
brahma angakānti tānra, mantra 15
śhūnyāyitam jagat sarvam, mantra 17

Hitopadesh
āhāra nidrā bhaya, mantra 15

Panchadashi
mana eva manuṣhyāṇām, mantra 13
tatpādāmburu hadvandva sevā, mantra 13

Panchatantra
yathā kharaḥ chandana, mantra 9

Shiv Mahimna Stotra
asita-giri-samam, Shanti Path Mantra

Saints, Devotees, and Philosophers

Chanakya Pandit, *Chanakya Neeti*
noluko 'pyavalokate yadi, mantra 6

Charvak, *Siddhant*
jaḍabhūtavikāreṣhu chaitanyam, mantra 9
trayovedasya kartārau, mantra 9
yāvajjīvet sukham jīvet, mantra 9

Saint Kabir
rāma rahe bana bhītare, mantra 13

Kalidas, *Kumarsambhava*
śharīram ādyam khalu, mantra 10

Jagadguru Kripaluji Maharaj, *Radha Govind Geet*
jaga men raho aise, mantra 14

Sage Narad

Narad Bhakti Darshan
īśhvarasyāpyabhimāndveṣhitvāt, mantra 5
kṣhaṇādharmapi vyartham na, mantra 2
tatprāpya tadevāvalokayati, mantra 7

Narad Pancharatra
deha-dehī-bhidā chaiva, mantra 8

Shankaracharya
yāvat gururna kartavyo, mantra 13

Ishopanishad Bhashya

asuryāḥ paramātmabhāvamadvayamapekṣhya, mantra 3

Brahma Sutra Bhashya

paśhvādibhiḥ chāviśheṣhāt, mantra 1

Bhaja Govindam

kā te kāntā kaste putraḥ, mantra 12

punarapi jananam punarapi maraṇam, mantra 11

Prabodh Sudhakar

śhuddhyati hi nāntarātmā, mantra 15

Vachaspati Mishra, *Bhamati Teeka*

smitametasya charācharamasya, mantra 4

Let's Connect

If you enjoyed reading this book and would like to connect with Swami Mukundananda, you can do so through any of the following channels:

Websites: *www.jkyog.org, www.jkyog.in, www.swamimukundananda.org*

YouTube: 'Swami Mukundananda' and 'Swami Mukundananda Hindi'

Apps: Bhagavad Gita Krishna Bhakti and Swami Mukundananda

Facebook: 'Swami Mukundananda' and 'Swami Mukundananda Hindi'

Instagram: 'Swami Mukundananda' and 'Swami Mukundananda Hindi'

Pinterest: Swami Mukundananda - JKYog

Telegram: Swami Mukundananda

X: Swami Mukundananda (@Sw_Mukundananda)

LinkedIn: Swami Mukundananda

Audio Podcasts: Apple, SoundCloud, Spotify

JKYog Radio: TuneIn app for iOS and Android

WhatsApp Daily Inspirations: We have two broadcast lists. You are welcome to join either or both.

India: +91 84489 41008
USA: +1 346-239-9675

Online Classes:

JKYog India: *www.jkyog.in/online-sessions/*
JKYog US: *www.jkyog.org/online-classes*